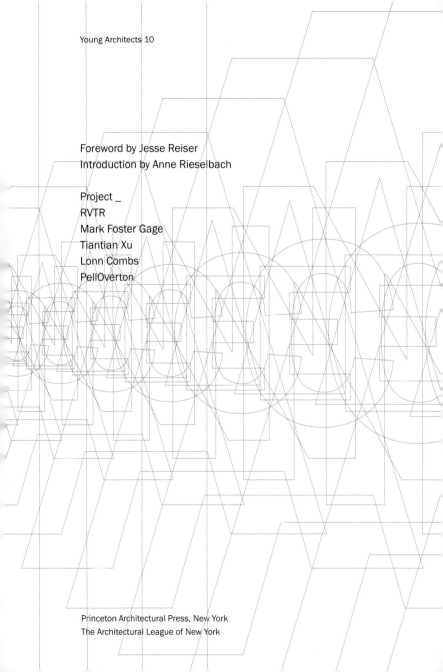

Young Architects 10

Foreword by Jesse Reiser
Introduction by Anne Rieselbach

Project _
RVTR
Mark Foster Gage
Tiantian Xu
Lonn Combs
PellOverton

Princeton Architectural Press, New York
The Architectural League of New York

Published by
Princeton Architectural Press
37 East Seventh Street
New York, New York 10003

For a free catalog of books, call 1.800.722.6657.
Visit our website at www.papress.com.

This publication is made possible with public funds from the New York State Council on the Arts, a
state agency.

State of the Arts

NYSCA

Editor: Lauren Nelson Packard
Designer: Jan Haux

Special thanks to: Nettie Aljian, Bree Apperley, Sara Bader, Nicola Bednarek, Janet Behning, Becca
Casbon, Carina Cha, Penny (Yuen Pik) Chu, Carolyn Deuschle, Russell Fernandez, Pete Fitzpatrick,
Wendy Fuller, Clare Jacobson, Aileen Kwun, Nancy Eklund Later, Linda Lee, Laurie Manfra, John
Myers, Katharine Myers, Dan Simon, Jennifer Thompson, Paul Wagner, Joseph Weston, and Deb
Wood of Princeton Architectural Press
—Kevin C. Lippert, publisher

Library of Congress Cataloging-in-Publication Data
Resonance / the Architectural League of New York ; foreword by Jesse Reiser ; introduction by Anne
Rieselbach. — 1st ed.
p. cm. — (Young architects ; 10)
ISBN 978-1-56898-809-2 (pbk. : alk. paper)
1. Young Architects Forum—Exhibitions. 2. Architecture—Awards—United States. 3. Architecture—
United States—History—21st century. 4. Young architects—United States. 5. Architecture and
society. I. Architectural League of New York.
NA2340.Y6798 2009
720.92—dc22
                                                                              2008051948

Contents

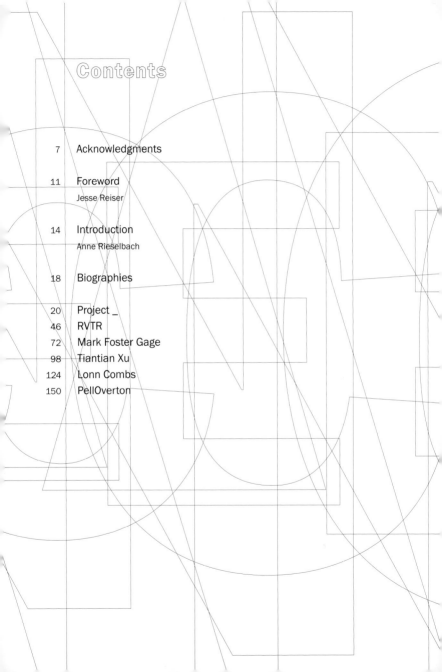

Architectural League Board of Directors

Acknowledgments

Calvin Tsao, President
The Architectural League of New York

The Young Architects Forum, now in its twenty-seventh season, continues to identify some of the most interesting contemporary work being created by young architects and designers. Open to architects and designers who are ten years or fewer out of undergraduate or graduate school, this annual portfolio competition's winnerse are given the opportunity to create site-specific installations of their work, present lectures at the League's Young Architects Forum, participate in video podcast interviews, as well as publish their work for this annual catalog.

The annual competition theme is developed by the Young Architects Committee—a group comprised of recent Young Architects Forum participants—and changes every year to reflect current issues in architectural design and theory. Its members, along with prominent members of the architecture and design community, serve as jurors.

I would like to thank this year's committee members Julie Beckman, Chris Lasch, and Jonathan Lott for the time and expertise they devoted to composing the competition theme and accompanying text. It was intriguing to hear their informed opinions alongside those of my fellow jurors Karen Fairbanks, Mark Robbins, and Jesse Reiser, who has also written the foreword to this publication. I also want to thank Michael Bierut and Jennifer Kinon for the competition graphics and Adam Mosseri, who transformed and animated their graphic language for installation onto the League's website. Photographer David Sundberg once again artfully documented the exhibition.

The Young Architects Forum is made possible in part by the generous support of Dornbracht, Susan Grant Lewin Associates, and Tischler und Sohn. The League's programs are also made possible in part by public funds from the New York City Department of Cultural Affairs and the New York State Council on the Arts, a State Agency. Finally, we also gratefully wish to acknowledge the support of the LEF Foundation for this publication.

Inertia

Jesse Reiser

It is an astonishing fact that the discipline of architecture, despite the relentless expansion of the profession, has steadfastly maintained an essentially steady state for the past five hundred years in terms of the number of architects who, in any generation, have made original and significant contributions; this, despite the spread of universal education, globalization, and the sheer volume of building in the world. If we take the last century as a measure, we are witness to the increasing inertia of architectural innovation. On the occasion of the sixtieth anniversary of the International Style exhibition at MoMA, Philip Johnson observed that in 1933 had he projected back sixty years to 1873, he would have been confronted with a panorama of hopelessly antique projects. Not so, he observed, from the vantage point of 1993, at which time the Modern architecture from 1933 still looked fresh and modern. So, post-Alberti, architecture has been practiced at the highest level by a small number of people on a limited number of recalcitrant models governed by the laws of inertia.

The inertia problem, however, may not be a problem at all. Certainly architecture has not been sped up, but undoubtedly slowed down, through gradualist research-based approaches. The apparent success of research, most pointedly exemplified today in certain Dutch practices, is a phenomenon more properly attributable to office propaganda, to the sociology of architect/client relations in the Low Countries, than of architecture itself. It is doubtful research specifically patterned on the scientific method has ever in reality sustained architectural projects in the first place. Good architects certainly experiment, but it is unclear that such knowledge is susceptible to the verification procedures of science. My friend Jeffrey Kipnis asks, "Was there ever an instance of architectural research that was famous for having failed?" Are negative results that definitively close down an avenue of speculation possible in architecture as they are in the sciences? We can either characterize our profession negatively as the practice of an absurdly soft science or, dare I say it, affirmatively as an art or, better still, *the* art. Now before I am assailed by a storm of protest from LEED-certified types or even some (most) of my colleagues and students, I would like to briefly relate my experience of a period of exceptional experimentation and innovation.

Having had the luck and the privilege to work with and compete against a formidable group of colleagues and students in the 1990s, it was clear to all that while the architectural problems, models, and legacies had been percolating for quite some time, the insights that prompted the resulting period of invention came about with startling rapidity and seemingly everywhere at once (another instance of inertia). It was certainly the farthest thing from the gradual stockpiling of disinterested research—more like the gold rush and the race to claim new territory first. Out of this feast, the Modernism Johnson celebrated was neither radically overthrown nor was it subject to minor material, regional, or mannerist, alterations. Rather the revaluation extended the project so far and so deeply that the canonical projects of Modernism could for the first time be seen in a new light; not as unsurpassable exemplars, from which anything after was a weaker derivative, but as special cases in a suddenly wider universe of possibilities.

It is widely assumed that the computer made possible the work of the nineties but this is only a partial truth. Certainly the new technologies made possible linkages between design, production, and economics that had never before existed, but the real breakthroughs were conceptual and cultural before they were technological. The same could be said for the current infatuation with scripting, where in the name of bespoke algorithms, as opposed to software borrowed from other disciplines, practitioners hope for an architecture that will be at long last more fully intentional, tractable, and rigorous. To be sure, scripting is certainly a useful addition to the toolbox. But in the worst case it becomes a substitute for active judgement. Inertia takes over and architects fool themselves into thinking that repetition—simple or complex—is a form of rational thought.

When Piranesi called into question the classical orders, architecture lost the guarantee of reason that the orders once bestowed axiomatically (a radical insight against origins that should give the scripters pause). The architect faced a real crisis of meaning. Piranesi's doubt initiated a new freedom and with it anxiety. If the presuppositions to a reasonable architecture could no longer be ordained, then perhaps reason could be found in the process. And if process is to be reasonable then the starting point becomes all important. But what guarantees a reasonable starting point? If we examine the timeworn categories of site, program, materials, needs, etc., we realize that they might all be otherwise—the maw of arbitrariness is opening, pulling us in. For better or worse, we must come to grips with the fact that arbitrariness is the medium in which architects swim. In the final analysis, a proper starting point, i.e., the questions of where we come from (where we begin) and where we are going (where we end), is a metaphysical question and is not knowable. Nor is it particularly important in terms of advancing a speculative project. Indeed, as Roland Barthes used to say, one can begin a project anywhere—there exists no privileged locus or time.

Open-ended research and process-based arguments are two sides of the same historical coin. Better to eschew the twin traps of memory (history) or dreams (research with realization infinitely deferred). What is in front of you is all you have. The project must advance from there. Sanford Kwinter likes to relate that apropos of writing: it is necessary to write yourself into a problem in order to write yourself out of it—that this is what motivates invention and brings forth the new. So too with architecture, there is an immediacy to this mode of working which is neither a backwards nor a forwards project, but an engagement with the here and now, a radical empiricism that has nothing to do with the everyday or maintaining the status quo.

The details—the fleshing out of avenues of development opened up in the 1990s and certainly the technology to move those insights into building practice have taken years to refine and are still in process today. In this sense, the time it takes to work through and even exhaust common themes and problems in architecture is not reducible to the technology that delivers it. It is no accident that the period of time of this last outpouring almost exactly equals the period of time from the High Renaissance to Mannerism—yet another aspect of the steady state condition. Cultural duration is in this sense neither historically nor technologically determined. We're now in a period of consolidation after more than a decade of rapid-fire invention. Projects and participants have matured so the inertia has swung toward the retrograde side of the equation; but the plus side of all this is that the buildings we'll see will be better and there is much for the next generation to take up.

Introduction

Anne Rieselbach

How can architects align the ambitions and capabilities of their discipline to address the needs and desires of a changing world? The Young Architects Committee challenged entrants to examine the means and methods of design practice through a series of probing questions which asked architects to reconsider their practices in light of the increased productivity enabled by technological advances in building methodologies, expanded communications networks, and cross-fertilization from other disciplines. The committee asked entrants to demonstrate ways contemporary architectural ideas and practice could meaningfully address issues and concerns outside the discipline.

The winning work resonates beyond the bounds of traditional architectural practice in differing ways. All six winners work within interdisciplinary practices that, in various combinations, synthetically engage communication, collaboration, and education, as well as programmatic and technological innovation to create unique architecture and design. From innovative modes of construction and repurposed building materials, to new definitions—virtual and real—of site, to new ways of visualizing information, the winning firms have expanded traditional geographic and methodological boundaries of architectural practice.

This year's winners took divergent routes to convey the character and impact of their work. Through their competition portfolios and then, more significantly, through the exhibition, they took full advantage of the opportunity to explicate, frame, and embody the ideas underlying their designs. In their creative hands, the interpretive possibilities inherent in tangibly visualizing their design process amplified the resonance of the work.

Enacting the interdisciplinary nature of their practice, Ana Miljacki and Lee Moreau of Project_ created take-away posters featuring their firm's design and research, as well as questions for visitors. The architects saw the exhibit as an opportunity to provoke conversation among their peers. The posters, displayed on cardboard plinths, fold down for recycling, intended to appeal to the audience's "taste for guerilla action...even possibly inhabiting other architectural books, journals, stores." The architects describe the "final image of the exhibit (the one we are dreaming up)...as the exhibit depleted to zero, after which we pack up the stands knowing that some images of our work and some portion of our verbal instigation still have a life somewhere else."

With their multimedia presentation, Geoffrey Thün and Kathy Velikov sought "to engage visitors in a state of attentiveness—whether aurally, through the moving image, through the turning of a page, or through a complex diagram of interrelationships." The installation, dominated by an intricate constellation of diagrams set on a brilliant blue field, mapped the formal, theoretical, and pragmatic aspects of their work. Below the field of diagrams, four videos embedded in a glass tabletop isolated the architects' principal matters of concern, such as "future ecologies, emerging inhabitations, and situated infrastructures," as well as the overarching conceptual and collective aspects of the firm's practice as visualized through a commissioned animation.

Mark Foster Gage described his firm Gage/Clemenceau Architects' image-packed display as based on Sir John Soane's Dulwich Picture Gallery in its pictorial arrangement, providing a broad, rather than deep, impression of the firm's work. The viewer achieved a general idea of their designs, from the image-packed display, but with no concrete details, it provided "an enticement toward curiosity." The centerpiece, their recent competition entry for the Estonian Academy of the Arts, was illustrated at varied scales—from a prototype wall panel and renderings to a shimmering mirrored model which, in turn, reflected and abstracted images of other projects including their entries for the Stockholm Public Library and P.S.1 competitions as well as their built residential projects.

Tiled images provided multiple views of Tiantian Xu's built work. Her firm DnA Design and Architecture's commissions include the Ordos Art Museum, Xiaopu Culture Center and Jinhua Architecture Park Public Toilet. Xu anchored each collection of project images with a site plan, locating and describing each project, providing a visual reference point for groupings of intentionally small-scaled photographs. Her intent behind the collage of images was to let visitors experience her projects through multiple viewpoints in the landscape and during the shifting light of the day, to "more spontaneously engage with the content." Directly below the wall panel of completed work were similarly displayed current projects—three public activity centers. Again, the focus was to engage visitors with how the firm develops its designs.

Based on a traditional picture gallery—more particularly, the relationship between prosaic illustrations of built work and fantastical speculative architectural fantasies, such as those rendered for Sir John Soane by Joseph Gandy—the installation by Lonn Combs of EASTON+COMBS centered on a collection of images of built and proposed projects. The design allowed the juxtaposition "of the various scales and strategies of the work to foreground affiliations of surface, texture, and spatial moods found in the built work with the atmospheres created in the projected (speculated or rendered) work." Set below the images, giving a three-dimensional reading of the work, were models of the Mill Center for the Arts and the Gyeonggi-do Jeongok Prehistory Museum, and a portfolio which delineated individual projects through plans and construction details.

Ben Pell and Tate Overton created a compressed scale mockup for a future gallery installation. Their piece, entitled *Passive-Aggressive*, embodied the formal and material exploration that shapes much of their firm's work. The piece layered growing plants, images of natural forms, and wallpaper-like abstract patterns that play with flatness, thematic variation, and repetition. Over the duration of the exhibition, flowering peace lilies grew through a perforated Plexiglas screen printed with images of the plants and coursed over a mirrored pedestal planted in a field of floral images. The architects' intent was to demonstrate ways graphics might transcend representation to create three-dimensional performative media.

Architecture, as described in the call for entries, has the capacity to incorporate and act on multiple layers of information from a vast array of sources. The collection of winning work demonstrates fresh design approaches that resoundingly answered the call "to identify ideas, implemented or not, that leverage that capacity creatively and proactively in the world."

Biographies

Lonn Combs studied architecture at the University of Kentucky, where he received his first professional degree in architecture in 1992. He later received a post-professional degree at Columbia University in 2001. Lonn Combs co-founded EASTON+COMBS in 2002 with over ten years of professional experience in Germany, China, and the United States. In tandem with the founding of EASTON+COMBS, he began teaching design studios and has taught at Pratt Institute School of Architecture and City College of New York, and Cornell University. He is currently Adjunct Associate Professor of Architecture and the Assistant Chair of Undergraduate Architecture at Pratt Institute.

Mark Foster Gage is the co-founder, with Marc Clemenceau Bailly, of Gage/Clemenceau Architects. The firm is known for its synthesis of aesthetic innovations with advanced technologies, often enabled by collaborative research with the software and manufacturing industries. Gage/Clemenceau Architects was a winner of the AIA *New Practices* citation in 2006, and was a finalist in the Museum of Modern Art/P.S.1 *Young Architects Program* in 2007. Mark Foster Gage is an Assistant Professor of Architecture and chair of the design curriculum at Yale University. He has also taught at Columbia University, at the Institute for Classical Architecture in New York, and has lectured internationally.

Ben Pell and Tate Overton founded PellOverton in New York City in 2005. The office is guided by an interest in blending research and practice through the exploration of innovative material applications and fabrication techniques. Ben Pell received his Master of Architecture from UCLA and his Bachelor of Architecture from Syracuse University. Ben has taught at the Pratt Institute and Syracuse University, and is currently on the faculty at the Yale School of Architecture. He is a Registered Architect in the State of New York. Tate Overton received his Bachelor of Architecture from the University of Kentucky, and has extensive experience in residential and commercial construction management and supervision.

Ana Miljacki and Lee Moreau founded the design and research firm Project_ in 1998. Through the production of buildings, exhibitions, writing, and the instigation of discourse, Project_ strives to critically engage and reimagine the contemporary world. Project_ relies on research to frame a particular problem and determine the most effective role for design. Both Ana Miljacki and Lee Moreau received their Bachelors degrees from Bennington College and their Master of Architecture degrees from Rice University. Ana completed her PhD in the History and Theory of Architecture at Harvard University. She is currently an assistant professor of architecture at MIT.

Kathy Velikov received her professional degree from the University of Waterloo and a Masters in History of Art and Architecture from the University of Toronto. She is a licensed architect and is currently Academic Committee Chair at the CaGBC. Geoffrey Thün received a Masters of Urban Design from the University of Toronto, his professional degree in Architecture from the University of Waterloo, and a Bachelor of Sociology from the University of Western Ontario. RVTR was founded by Velikov and Thün along with partners Colin Ripley and Paul Raff and is driven by the belief that the manner in which we develop our landscapes and build our cities is critical to our collective global future.

Tiantian Xu is founding principal of Design and Architecture Beijing (DnA Beijing), an interdisciplinary practice for city planning, urban design, and architecture. Xu received her Master of Architecture in Urban Design from the Harvard Graduate School of Design in 2000, and her Bachelors in Architecture from Tsinghua University in Beijing. Prior to establishing DnA Beijing, she worked at a number of design firms in the United States and the Netherlands. She has also taught at the Central Academy of Fine Arts (CAFA) School of Architecture. in Beijing, and has been a guest critic in numerous schools including Peking University and Tokyo Chiba Institute of Technology. She received a WA China Architecture Award in 2006.

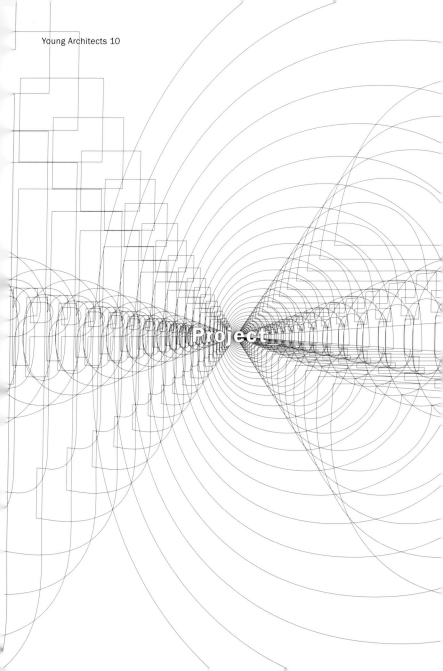

Project

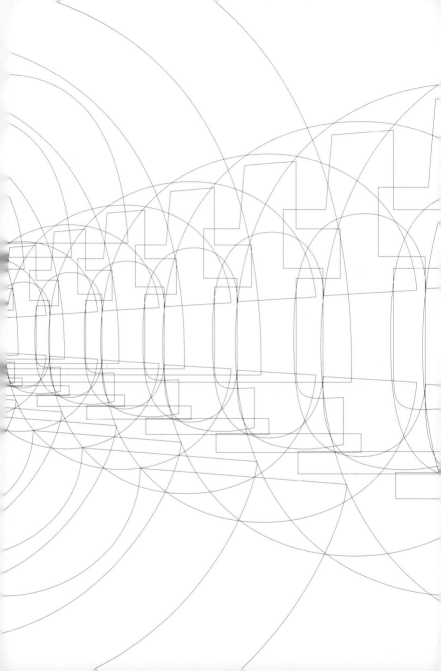

Torino, Italy 2008
Exhibition with Benjamin Porto and Daniel Sakai

We were invited by Francesco Bonami and the Fondazione Sandretto Re Rebaudengo in Turin to contribute a prison cell design to their YouPrison exhibit, together with twelve other international architects. After researching reform ideas within the U.S. prison system, prison labor laws, as well as the actual architectural implications of a cell redesign, we decided to dedicate our exhibition to explicating the dilemma that a designer finds himself in when asked to impact (through the design of a room) a system determined by agents and agencies well beyond any architect's domain.

As a direct result of recent legislation and of the general cultural embrace of "cleaning up" and normalizing American cities, the number of individuals in U.S. prisons has been steadily increasing, which has brought clear financial benefit to private prison management companies over the last decade. The interior of U.S. prisons is also one of the last sites of production in an otherwise post-industrial economy. None of this is to say that prisons do not involve architectural design— on the contrary, prison architectures often survive the governments that sponsor them—but rather, to begin to describe the intricate and vast network of agents involved in the shaping of the U.S. correctional system in order to understand what possible agency an architect might have in this situation. Not only is the contemporary architect not the same figure as the eighteenth-century reformer/architect, but the cell is in fact too small a unit of carceral space to impact the deeply problematic structures and practices that extend well beyond it today.

The floor of our installation is an informational display that requires the visitor to perform our research and our dilemma spatially. Three main voices are reconstructed: the voice of the legislature and governmental agencies, the voice of all who benefit from the prison system financially, and the voice of the prisoners. Each of these agents spins the information in specific ideological directions. Although it may be possible to care about only one of these larger agents, the

1   Gallery Installation

connections between them are intricate, inextricably woven together, and, most importantly, entangle the figure of the architect as well.

Above the large informational display, an illuminated polypropylene cell is presented upside down, as an invitation to contemplate architectural design. If the floor invites one to try to understand the network of agents involved in the prison industrial system or in this contemporary species of prisoner reform, the upper portion of the installation presents a limit case scenario, based on plausible future outcomes of current trends in prison management and contemporary culture. Starting with the ongoing increase in skilled and non-violent prisoner populations, our scenario involves the possible expansion of prison reform arguments to embrace ideas about the special (reform) value of creative work.

1

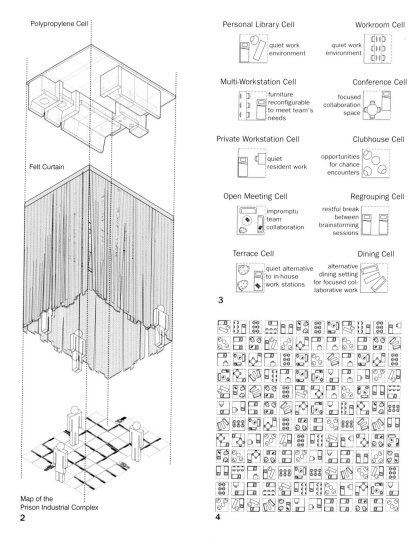

Polypropylene Cell

Felt Curtain

Map of the
Prison Industrial Complex

2

Personal Library Cell

quiet work
environment

Multi-Workstation Cell

furniture
reconfigurable
to meet team's
needs

Private Workstation Cell

quiet
resident work

Open Meeting Cell

impromptu
team
collaboration

Terrace Cell

quiet alternative
to in-house
work stations

Workroom Cell

quiet work
environment

Conference Cell

focused
collaboration
space

Clubhouse Cell

opportunities
for chance
encounters

Regrouping Cell

restful break
between
brainstorming
sessions

Dining Cell

alternative
dining setting
for focused col-
laborative work

3

4

5   Polypropylene Cell Assembly Drawing
6   Life in the Live/Work Cell

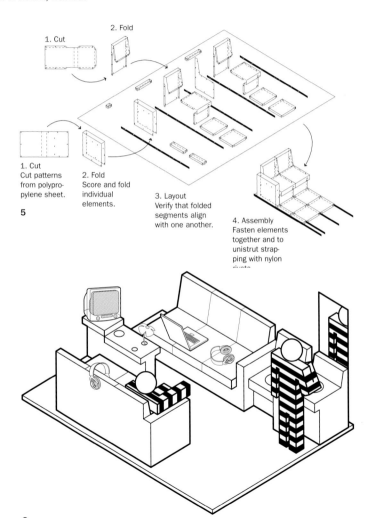

2. Fold

1. Cut

1. Cut
Cut patterns
from polypro-
pylene sheet.

2. Fold
Score and fold
individual
elements.

5

3. Layout
Verify that folded
segments align
with one another.

4. Assembly
Fasten elements
together and to
unistrut strap-
ping with nylon
rivets.

7   Floor Graphics Presenting Our Research on
        the Prison Industrial Complex

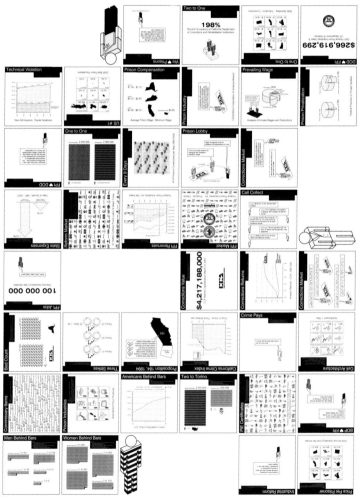

8   View Inside Gallery Installation

Hi! Park

Belgrade, Serbia 2008
Competition Entry

The Society of Serbian Architects organized a competition for the redesign of an important park at the confluence of the Sava and Danube
rivers. The park in question, colloquially called "confluence," but in the
literature of the competition referred to as the "Park of Friendship,"
was planned into existence at the early stages of the postwar development of New Belgrade, which is Belgrade's largest communist-era
planned housing development. We set our goals in this competition on
two registers very specific to the Serbian context. One involved an ear-
nest desire to find a way to preserve the park, to allow for an approach
to the river that has in recent years been hampered and nearly
destroyed by a semi-legal economy of entertainment rafts, while still
finding a way to allow for that microeconomy to somehow dock. The
other goal was to inject some humor and debate into the extremely
professionalized architectural discourse in Serbia. We thought this lat-
ter goal required humor and low-resolution, but high IQ explanations.

 Working from a basic programmatic survey of the situation and
a fundamental belief that all contemporary definitions of nature rely
on a type of construction, we proposed six zones that differ from one
another in terms of the relationship between the human activities and
the treatment of nature. Our proposal employed six different programmatic and related formal strategies: bunching, seeding, combing,
scooping, packing, sampling.

1   Existing Conditions
2   Proposed Vegetation and Paths

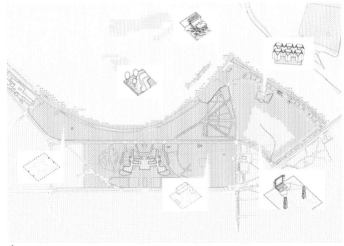

1

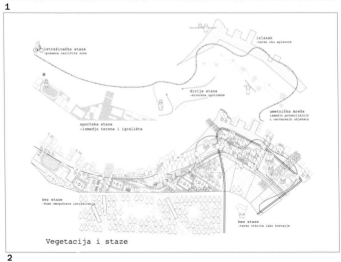

Vegetacija i staze

2

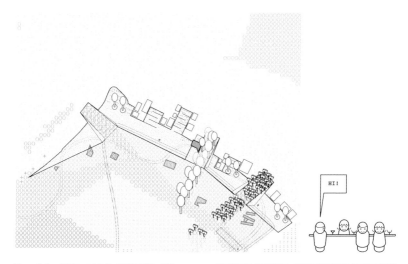

Zone 1, in which we are bunching the rafts, provides areas in direct relation to the water and is formally resolved such that it allows rafts to connect while ensuring openings that cannot be occupied by rafts for views and access to the water on foot.

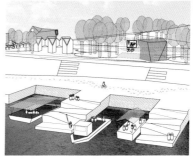

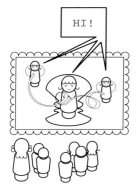

Zone 2 is programmatically dedicated to cultural and artistic content, as it is currently the site of the famous postwar building of the museum of contemporary art. We intensified Zone 2 through a network of paths, clearings for future art and cultural buildings and circularly shaped forests. We called this formal maneuver seeding.

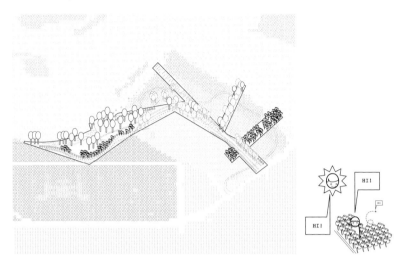

Zone 3 is entirely constructed wilderness. It profits from existing riverbanks and flood areas where some still go fishing. No paths, no benches, only grasses, trees, mud, all formally combed in such a way that each subzone is defined by the life and morphology of plants.

Zone 4 is located in the area that has often been used in recent years for large pop concerts. We propose to scoop the concert visitors through a land/landscaping gesture, which focuses that portion of the park towards the back of the proposed location of the new opera building. The lifted landscape allows for a new parking facility underneath.

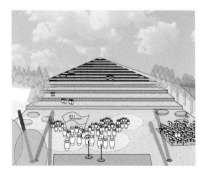

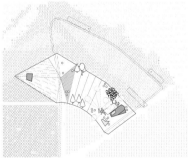

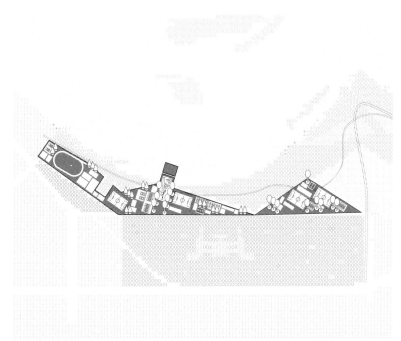

Zone 5 is dedicated to sport playgrounds; it packs together tennis, basketball, mini soccer, and bocce courts, producing a topographically activated but brutally rationalized landscape of play, spectatorship, and occasional shade, all connected by a running and biking turf.

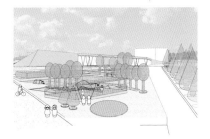

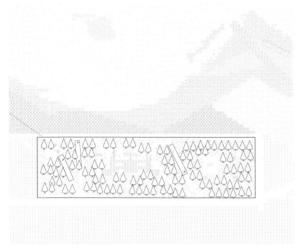

Zone 6 contains within it the old, modernist, imposing and impressive building of the old executive branch of the communist party as well as a foundation for the never completed Museum of the Revolution. We propose here to plant a dense forest, which would overtake the grand paved paths and reframe this part of our history as nature and as a piece of historical memory.

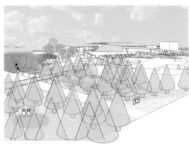

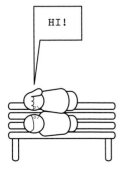

Project_insert

New York, New York 2008

Building on the spirit of this year's Young Architects Forum, we designed Project_insert to serve as our exhibition and as another probe to send out into the world. Project_insert invites all visitors to the Young Architects exhibit to participate in the guerilla dissemination of some of our work and ideas by taking copies and literally inserting them in books, magazines, libraries, and bookstores. We were particularly interested in collecting answers to our questionnaire for young architects, which we see as an important generational project that will have a life beyond the exhibition. Apart from our ambition to instigate further discourse with Project_insert, and to circulate some of our work and our students' work, we imagined Project_insert literally setting up a type of reciprocity between dissemination and the gallery space. As the stacks of this take away mini-journal were depleted in the gallery, we imagined our ideas and work beginning their journey into the city.

1   Insert Action Diagram   **2–3** Exhibition Photographs

1. Fold Center   2. Fold Again   3. Fold To Go   Take...   Keep...   ...or Insert

Please take one of each to keep or ...insert it somewhere smart.

1

2   3

4

5

6

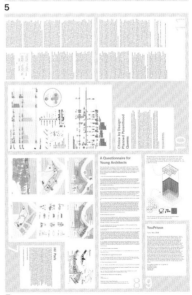

7

Studio 24b

Portland, Maine 2006

Studio 24b was one of those design opportunities that came with no money and a very self-motivated client. We were asked to design a woodshop and a painting studio in Maine, which together had to pose as a garage and occasionally function as a gallery. It was a mischievous project from the outset and also one that had to work on the ground, logistically, not only as a final product, but also as a carefully thought out construction process that eventually involved numerous volunteers.

We thought that if we engaged architecturally the identity of the users and of the identity of the garage that Studio 24b represented on its permit papers, we could produce something functional and unique in the context of Portland's fringes. The architectural solution of Studio 24b features a continuously changing section that makes the woodshop inevitably different from the painting studio while keeping them coherently synthesized in a single object. We used revolving walls in place of doors, which ensures a garage reading from one angle, while it enables the painting studio and the gallery to spill outside. The non-standard use of standard residential construction techniques made the assembly relatively easy for its amateur construction crews and ensured it minor landmark status in its neighborhood of Portland, Maine. The collective construction of the building brought the neighbors closer together and has instigated improvements along the entire block of adjacent properties.

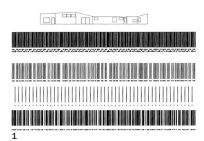

1

2

3

4

5

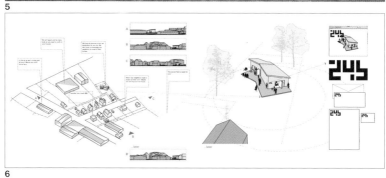

6

7   Plan and Elevations

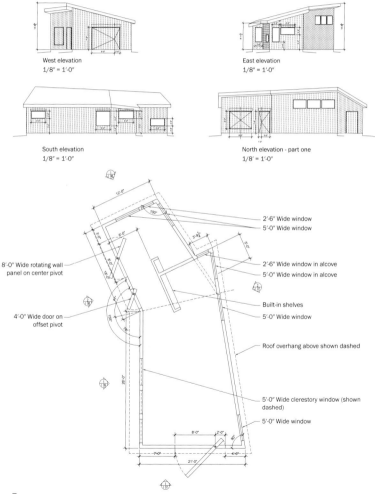

West elevation
1/8″ = 1'-0″

East elevation
1/8″ = 1'-0″

South elevation
1/8″ = 1'-0″

North elevation - part one
1/8' = 1'-0″

8'-0″ Wide rotating wall
panel on center pivot

4'-0″ Wide door on
offset pivot

2'-6″ Wide window
5'-0″ Wide window

2'-6″ Wide window in alcove
5'-0″ Wide window in alcove

Built-in shelves
5'-0″ Wide window

Roof overhang above shown dashed

5'-0″ Wide clerestory window (shown
dashed)

5'-0″ Wide window

8   9

10

11

The Architects of Our Happiness

Prague, Belgrade, Warsaw 2005-2006
Research Project with Luke Bulman and Kimberly Shoemake

Fascinated by the vast landscape of the post-wall transition and with
the Graham Foundation's sponsorship, we embarked on this ambitious documentary project. 170,000,000 people reportedly live in the
communist-era housing of Eastern Europe and Russia. We wanted to
record and make some sense of these deeply ideological architectures, their massive scale, the entropic breakdown of the society that
produced them, and the industrious (and no less strange) capitalist
makeover that was taking place on the same vast scale. We visited
housing districts of Warsaw, Prague, and Belgrade to record this landscape in transition, aesthetically awesome (in all senses of that word),
brutal, relentless, and nearly beautiful on its own terms.

     We titled the project "The Architects of Our Happiness" after
a mock documentary imbedded in the 1971 film *Man of Marble* by
Andrzej Wajda. We organized our findings into six categories of phenom-
ena. *170,000,000* contained large architectural formations, building
configurations, and the sky figured between them. *Pazi Metak!* which in
Serbian means "watch out for bullets," contained all the open spaces
we found between things, some considered, some not. The name for
this section came from a billboard we found in one of the open spaces
of New Belgrade in Serbia, which just before New Year's Eve reminded
inhabitants of one of the functions of the open spaces between housing.
Pastels concentrated on the hues and contrasts we found; it included
the greys of Belgrade and the newly insulated (with dryvit) and freshly
painted (formerly grey) housing stock from Warsaw and Prague. The
category *Good Year* was constituted out of all kinds of commercial
language, oversized, profane, loud, that was not initially planned and
installed in the housing districts we visited, thus still a bit awkward and
surreal when we recorded it. *11Jan* was a category that collected all the
small events and traces of daily life in the housing districts. And lastly,
Eye Sore was a Super 8 film we produced by taking a single shot every
time we saw Houston, Texas, in our Eastern European cities.

1   Stills from *Eye Sore* Film

1

2   Warsaw, Poland   **3**   Prague, Czech Republic

Good Year. The language of commercialism

The entire landscape of Eastern Europe is sprinkled with oversized billboards that seem to watch over the housing districts like freshly made-up shopping fairies. Some form of commercial activity was always imagined to support the housing districts, but for many the transition to capitalism has meant the importation of a truly international exurbia—consisting of anything from KFC to IKEA.

With the sprawling commercial world on one side and the shopping malls on the other, these billboards could almost seem natural, if not for their awkward search for the right scale. And if we were to reverse engineer them, we might learn something that we were already suspecting about the vast open spaces of the modernist housing districts: words and images project far here. After all, this was the world in which production was propelled by propaganda, and consumption was meant to balance out necessity.

Pastels. The coloring of prefab concrete

In the summer of 2005, Przyzolek Grochowski, a housing estate dating from 1968–1974, was visibly falling apart from neglect, but its exterior hallways and pattern of protruding "rest" balconies still appeared the way Zofia and Oskar Hansen had designed them. Open form in architecture—with all of its period resonance and references—was Hansen's brain child and

4   Warsaw, Poland   **5**   Prague, Czech Republic

is evidenced in this project by the "elevated streets" at the courtyard edge of
every floor. Przyzolek Grochowski had
its problems of course, but compared
to the vast majority of mass housing
examples in Warsaw, it was considered aesthetically and had managed
to test radical typological innovations.
Recently, this estate began to receive
the treatment that has been spreading
across Poland and the Czech Republic
for several years. DRYVIT + PAINT. The
inhabitants are warmer, and Oskar
Hansen thinks the society is going
down the tubes.

*170,000,000. Building formations and
the shape of the sky*
Local specificity and difference, the
various forms of wilderness, and an
ever-shifting wash of "happiness"

cannot soften the relentless repetition
once the camera lens is zoomed out
far enough. And yet, at that scale—the
scale of total view—resides the pleasure of accessing totality, even if this is
merely an optical illusion.

After observing one of his typically
entropic sites of interest, Hotel
Palenque, Robert Smithson claimed
that the logic of the whole place was
"just impossible to fathom," that there
was no way that someone could possibly figure it out. This was, of course,
why he fell in love with it. Can one fall
in love with béton brut ad infinitum,
with long shadows, with triptych buildings, with 1960s residential skyscrap-
ers? When the light hits them just
right…they can be sublime. And for
170 million people they are all they

6   Warsaw, Poland   7   New Belgrade, Serbia

have ever known. We found an entropic landscape but instead of marvel-
ing at its otherness we thought that
perhaps we could discover how these
different architectures (and people)
formed in a non-consumer-consump-
tive society behave.

*Pazi Metak! Occupying the space
between things*
"Pazi Metak!" (Watch out for bullets!)
reads one of the billboards in New
Belgrade. A friendly reminder for every-
one. The ubiquitous modernist scale of
open space and the often self-referen-
tial disposition of buildings—carpeting
large territories of land with abstract
two dimensional patterns—gets rou-
tinely blamed for all of the stray bullets
(and accidental deaths) on New Year's
Eve. These celebratory shots soar

through the big empty spaces between
the blocks and, occasionally, fly
through windows killing other inhabitants of the district.

Not solely to blame, the vast voids
are structural to this landscape, and
can be the very essence of bucolic
(Warsaw) or completely unkempt,
sunburnt, and overgrown (Belgrade or
Prague). Many of the debates about
these housing estates beginning in
the 1970s centered on the need for
a human scale, both for the buildings
and for these open spaces, and typically involved overturning the Athens
Charter formula that prescribed them.

*11 January 2005. One day in the
housing blocks of New Belgrade*
As much as Godard's *Two or Three*

8 Warsaw, Poland

9 New Belgrade, Serbia

Things I Know About Her is a self-appointed critique of industrial society and stars the banlieux of Paris, Kristof Kieslowski's *Decalogue* series is a critique of the communist version of the industrial society presented under the guise of moral education. The housing block in *Decalogue* is not merely the organizing structure of the series; it is its main protagonist. The housing block has many eyes and many stories to tell and most importantly Kieslowski's series proposed that there is a unique logic of living in the housing blocks.

The daily life of the masses was a topic of great importance in all societies that claimed to have abolished the class system. The ideal proletarian masses would be fit, interested in culture, would shop optimally and be as hip as their western counterparts, but without obsessively caring about fashion. They would have charming offspring and, of course, ample leisure time to spend on sports and arts. Thus, sprinkled along the daily routes of New Belgrade's inhabitants, we find the social program and the infrastructure meant to support the utopian population inhabiting the residential architecture.

These mysterious lonely pavilions, regional schools and kindergartens, basketball hoops, and mini soccer fields are all still around, but the cultural centers seem to have given way to pubs, poker joints, shopping malls, and carnival grounds.

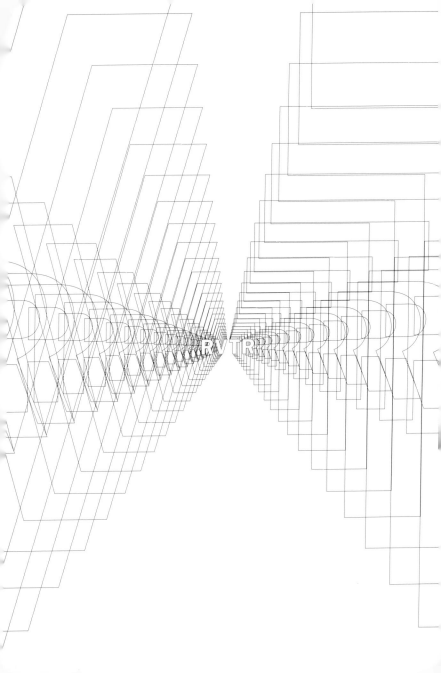

Buoyant Aquacology

The city of Venice marks the quintessential marriage of architecture and water. However, this relationship is a precarious one, sustained only through an immense technological and political tour de force. In an attempt to maintain the condition of the Venetian Lagoon, a condition of being neither land nor sea, military and defensive operations began, in the Renaissance, to alter the Lagoon's natural evolution, diverting two rivers from emptying fresh water and silt into it, and turning its waters increasingly saline.

In a future of radically rising sea levels, Venice risks becoming Atlantis. Architecture needs to be asking how we might build, live, operate and create societies within the reality of volatile and unpredictable weather, in a world of flooded cities, new deserts, cities the scale of small countries and collapsing ecosystems.

Venice could become a city protected from rising sea levels by great ringed barrier walls, with locks for access and trade. The Lagoon would become an arm of the sea, with new ecologies, and economies, supplanting those that have disappeared. A shifting matrix, a net, of floating energy barges will produce hydrogen algae to be farmed for energy production, as well as a food and mineral source, while processing sewage from the cities and using it to grow new soil. Other barges will support hydroponic agriculture, fish hatcheries, and solar collection cells. The northern portion of the island of Murano will become an ecological preserve where tidal flats and marshlands will be manufactured for study and preservation of marine species in a state of continuous succession, evolving through managed dynamic ecological processes, and through interaction with the new forces of sea. Individual floating vessels, controlled by a GPS information network, facilitate access to this new territory. These vessels take the form of transparent bubbles constructed of a chambered high performance skin, which allows unrestricted views of both the new life above and the cities submerged below the water line.

1   Lagoon Aquacology Plan

Project Team: Mark Friesner, Zhivka Hristova, Clayton Payer, Colin Ripley, Geoffrey Thün, Kathy Velikov

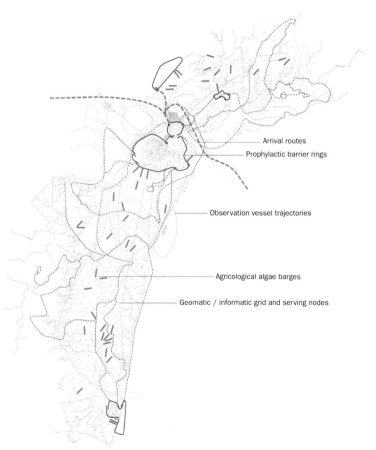

Arrival routes

Prophylactic barrier rings

Observation vessel trajectories

Agricological algae barges

Geomatic / informatic grid and serving nodes

2   Sacca San Mattia Park from Ecological Zone Toward Barrier Wall and Murano
3   Venice and Floating Observation Vessels in the Lagoon Park

2

3

4   Lagoon Prototypes: Strategies and Systems
5   Within Prophylactic Barrier: Interpretive Vessel
6   Atop Prophylactic Barrier: Infrastructural Viaduct

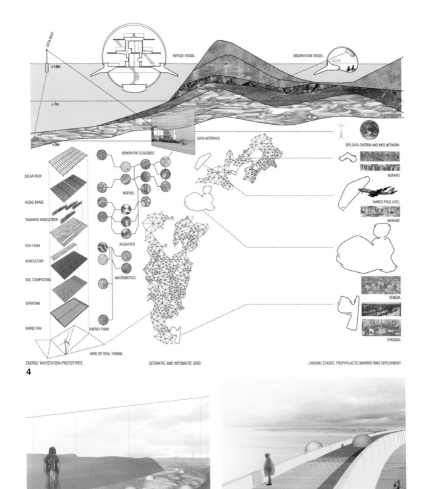

4

5   6

Post-Carbon Highway

This project explores the likely possibility that the depletion of carbon-based fuels will not precipitate a decline in mobility coupled with a corresponding demise of the automotive and transport industries, a collapse of global trade networks and perhaps even a return to small-scale recognizable and quantifiable city patterns, but rather, these conditions will become instrumental in reconceiving more efficiently and intensely connected regional urbanities and infrastructures.

The highway has arguably been the single most instrumental factor in structuring settlement patterns and economic development during the last half of the twentieth century. The post-carbon world will primarily entail the transformation from a plentiful single-sourced fuel to a more technologically advanced matrix of inputs from a variety of sources. The highway system will need to be re-evaluated and genetically redesigned to do more, becoming much more intelligent in the organization of goods, people, and energy along its length.

Instead of having the surface of the highway universally accessible to all vehicle types traveling at similar speeds, the highway could become differentiated to accommodate different vehicle types and speeds. Like multiplex cables, where multiple wavelengths of data can travel at variable speeds along the same line, the post-carbon highway accommodates a variety of transportation types and velocities. The network of parallel, cooperative modes of mobility include high speed rail, dedicated freight and vehicle lanes configured in a "thick" system where transport types are stacked and separated to maximize temporal efficiency, safety, and accessibility.

The multimodal transfer interchange will become the key node along the highway and the place where the highway and its travelers are able to interface with its dependent population concentrations. The strategic sites and available footprint for such interchanges are already determined by the logic of the existing system, in the vast orphaned spaces of interchange loops. In the post-carbon era of new fuels, a variety of refueling systems are provided at every service point, each fully integrated with the differentiated modes of travel. Freight transfer points complete with sorting and distribution capacity will facilitate the transfer of goods along the highway's length. Parking facilities, easily accessible to the transit interchange, encourage people to leave their cars and take advantage of faster and far more energy-efficient modes of travel. The transfer interchange also becomes a site for new services, shops, and entertainment for the people living in the multi-centered urban region. Fresh food terminals for local organic farmers, daycares, shopping centers, postal and courier stations attend these social condensers, connecting residents and businesses with the space of the post-carbon highway.

Project Team: Matt Peddie, Sonja Storey-Fleming, Matt Storus, Geoffrey Thün, Kathy Velikov

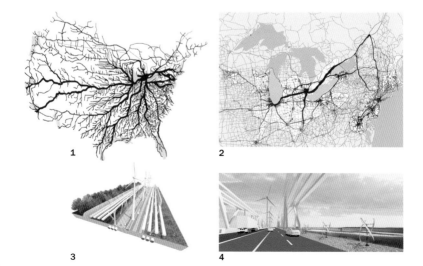

1

2

3

4

5   Multimodal Transfer Interchange: Flows and Uses
6   Multimodal Transfer Interchange: Bird's-Eye View

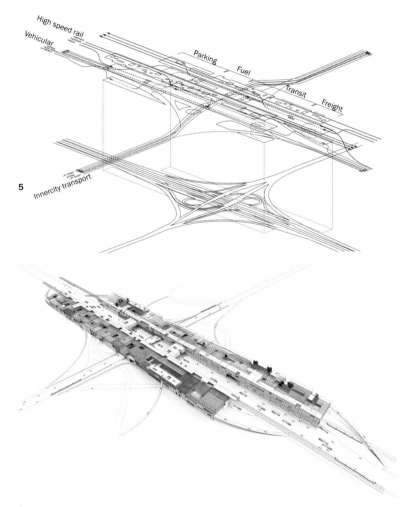

5

6

7   Multimodal Transfer Interchange: Freight Section
8   Multimodal Transfer Interchange: Transit Section

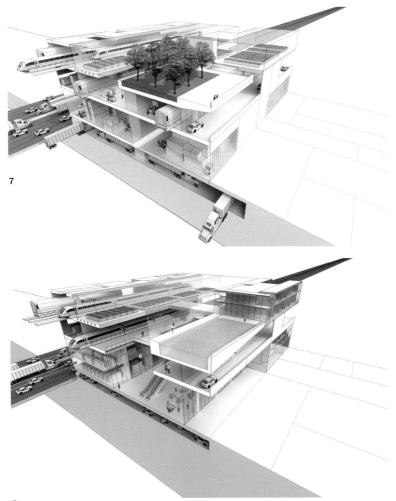

7

8

Nexus | Park | City

This development, located along the Yitong river on the outskirts of Changchun, proposes an alternate approach to the dominant type of gated single family subdivision development currently underway in China. The project intertwines a networked infrastructure of landscape types with housing, treating the built realm as part of an interrelated ecosystem that seeks to maximize the degree to which the built domain and its landscape might commingle and foster new types of relations among its inhabitants. Higher density housing allows for more of the land to be consolidated into significant areas that can support natural processes, for the management of site storm water, grey water, and for the production of ecological complexity and experiential delight.

A series of "fingers" connect the project's landscaped spaces with the adjacent regional network of the watershed. Inhabitants interact with this landscape and with their community through a series of continuous recreational circuits that offer a variety of active and passive opportunities for leisure within the public realm. Each East-West band is figured after a proto-typical regional ecosystem type, so although their performance is limited by dimension, they collectively form an internal microcosm of the broader regional structure, replete with a wide variety of flora and fauna. In order to foster the range of conditions necessary to support this diversity, extensive topographic operations refigure the existing flat terrain to generate a series of folds that can capture and retain water at a variety of depths and durations initiating and propelling vegetal differentiation. Specific planting configurations seed the succession model that minimizes active maintenance requirements while promising a rich tableau of conditions and experiences.

On the western edge of the project, the walled figure of the development is reinforced by a continuous elevated berm along which a variety of community programs are positioned. Each building

1   Site Topology

addresses the block exterior at grade, and relates to the internal landscape at the upper level. The housing is designed so as to modulate the extreme summer heat and winter cold experienced at 43° latitude. In addition to designing all buildings with high perform-ance envelopes, and energy efficiency gained from row housing, a range of building vocabularies are developed that respond to the solar orientation and adjacent urban space conditions of each type, allowing the array of facades that results to provide the architectural identity unique to specific locations within this matrix and direct access to the adjacent landscape network.

Project Team: Matt Peddie, Paul Raff, Colin Ripley, Sonja Storey-Fleming, Geoffrey Thün, Kathy Velikov

"Mogul Field" Wetland

Raised Deciduous Strip

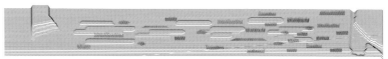

Park Landscape "Fingers"   Gradiated Grassland Swath

1

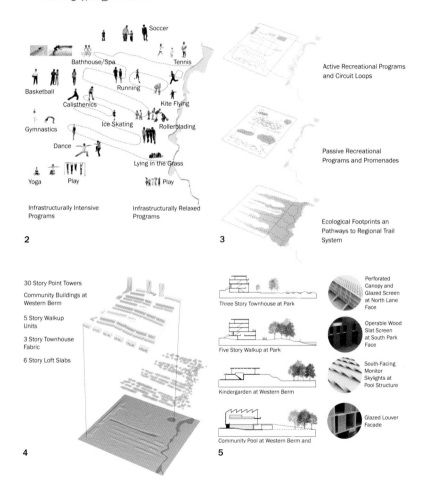

Soccer

Bathhouse/Spa

Tennis

Basketball

Running

Calisthenics

Kite Flying

Gymnastics

Ice Skating

Rollerblading

Dance

Lying in the Grass

Yoga   Play

Play

Infrastructurally Intensive
Programs

Infrastructurally Relaxed
Programs

2

Active Recreational Programs
and Circuit Loops

Passive Recreational
Programs and Promenades

Ecological Footprints an
Pathways to Regional Trail
System

3

30 Story Point Towers

Community Buildings at
Western Berm

5 Story Walkup
Units

3 Story Townhouse
Fabric

6 Story Loft Slabs

Three Story Townhouse at Park

Five Story Walkup at Park

Kindergarden at Western Berm

Community Pool at Western Berm and

Perforated
Canopy and
Glazed Screen
at North Lane
Face

Operable Wood
Slat Screen
at South Park
Face

South-Facing
Monitor
Skylights at
Pool Structure

Glazed Louver
Facade

4   5

6   Existing/Proposed Types
7   View at Northern Entry Gate
8   Park Promenade at Mogul Field Wetlands

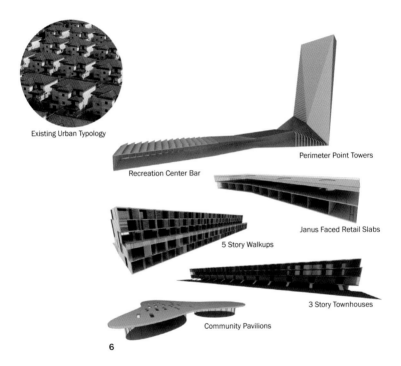

Existing Urban Typology

Perimeter Point Towers

Recreation Center Bar

Janus Faced Retail Slabs

5 Story Walkups

3 Story Townhouses

Community Pavilions

6

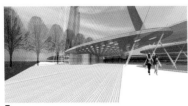

7

8

North House

North House is a prototype dwelling developed in response to the extreme conditions of northern climates, that pairs complete solar power with mobile and interactive technologies. The exterior layers of the house comprise a thick responsive envelope that physically mediates energy production, environmental conditions, and the personal comfort preferences of the occupants. A flexible distributed system of photovoltaic integrated louvers, roof panels, screens and fabrics generate solar energy, provide shading or access to the exterior, and are capable of mitigating extreme weather shifts. They close down when the house is in conditioned mode and open up to allow the house to breathe and expand during the temperate seasons.

The Adaptive Living Interface is a thin skin of information systems, responsive to touch, capable of subtle display, and able to mediate interactions between occupants and building systems. Touch-controlled interfaces and ambient cues create a tangible, physical involvement with the technologies and systems of the house. Technology is no longer cold and remote, but made personal and physical by developing ways that people can measure energy use with their own bodies. The system assists occupants in making informed decisions about energy by providing feedback on the energy state of the home. The home network is fully integrated with one's mobile phone, that indicates when the house has begun to produce surplus energy, and then allows one to choose and direct this energy to power up the battery of an electric vehicle or appliance, or sell energy to the global market via the grid. The occupant is at the centre, and in control of this environment, while both at home and away, connected through the now pervasive and ubiquitous net of global energy and information.

This project represents the most extensive collaborative undertaking within Canadian Architectural Academic history, and is being developed as an intensive collaboration between faculty and students at the University of Waterloo, Simon Fraser University's School of

1   North House in Rocky Mountains
2   Interior Perspective—Winter Morning (9:00am)
3   Interior Perspective—Summer Evening (8:00pm)

Interactive Arts and Technology, and Ryerson University. A prototypical version of North House will be constructed for, and compete in the U.S. Department of Energy's 2009 Solar Decathlon initiative.

Project Team: Philip Beesley, Lauren Barhydt, Chris Black, Eric Bury, Paul Cohoon, Michael Collins, Chloe Doesburg, Joe Dhanjal, Alan Fung, Johnathan Gammell, Egest Gjinali, Newsha Ghaeli, Mark Gorgolewski, Andrew Haydon, Haley Isaacs, Natalie Jackson, Jennifer Janzen, Laura Knap, Ivan Lee, Richard Lam, Kevin Lisoy, Bart Lowmanowski, Geordie Manchester, Dan McTavish, Davis Marques, Farid Noufailly, Matt Peddie, Spencer Rand, Kirsten Robinson, Damian Rogers, Adam Schwartzentruber, Amir Shahrokhi, Siva Sivothathaman, Sonja Storey-Fleming, Matt Storus, John Straube, Geoffrey Thün, Humphrey Tse, Kathy Velikov, Ron Wakkary, Tim Wat, Robert Woodbury, John Wright

1

2

3

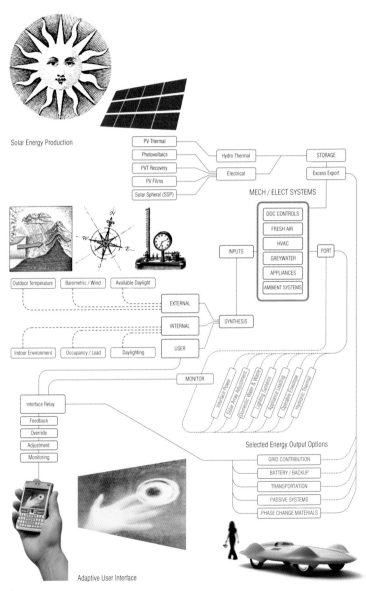

Solar Energy Production

PV Thermal
Photovoltaics
PVT Recovery
PV Films
Solar Spheral (SSP)

Hydro Thermal
Electrical

STORAGE
Excess Export

MECH / ELECT SYSTEMS

DDC CONTROLS
FRESH AIR
HVAC
GREYWATER
APPLIANCES
AMBIENT SYSTEMS

INPUTS

PORT

Outdoor Temperature   Barometric / Wind   Available Daylight

EXTERNAL

INTERNAL   SYNTHESIS

Indoor Environment   Occupancy / Load   Daylighting

USER

MONITOR

Interface Relay

Feedback
Override
Adjustment
Monitoring

Interface Power
Solar Array Adjustment
Domestic Water & Waste
Lighting Systems
Appliance Loading
Operable Envelope
Hydronic Thermal

Selected Energy Output Options

GRID CONTRIBUTION
BATTERY / BACKUP
TRANSPORTATION
PASSIVE SYSTEMS
PHASE CHANGE MATERIALS

Adaptive User Interface

5   Exploded Axonometric

6   North House Plan

4   Adaptive Living Interface Systems Diagram

7   North House Facade Study

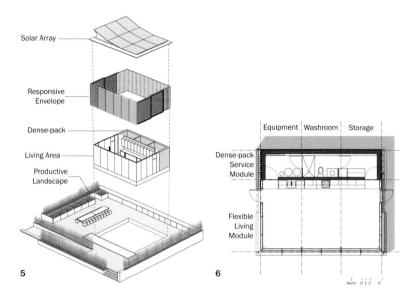

Solar Array

Responsive Envelope

Dense-pack

Living Area

Productive Landscape

5

Equipment | Washroom | Storage

Dense-pack Service Module

Flexible Living Module

6

North 0' 1' 2'   5'

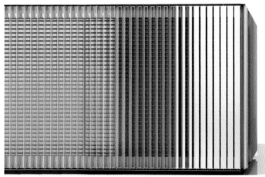

7

S.W.A.M.P. House

The Sustainable Weekend And Multi-Program House is located on a low lying property on the east side of the Lake Huron shore. The project was conceived of as a hovering luminous construct where the minimization of site impacts achieved through a range of architectonic and technological strategies manifest in an image of these priorities uniquely married with its wetland context.

The project consists of two primary volumes: pavilion and tower. The low-slung horizontal pavilion hovers on pilotis above the vegetal flow, permitting the soils of the coastal woodland to continue to filter surface water as it moves toward the lake. Its south face is glazed to frame a long foreground view across the clearing and into the woodlot. Passive solar and daylighting priorities are mediated by a set of advanced glazing treatments, generating a range of performative and phenomenal effects.

The tower houses the project's services at grade, consolidated beneath a stair that accesses an upper loft elevated above the surrounding vegetation, permitting distant views to the horizon. The south face of the tower is clad with photovoltaic film captured within a laminated glass rainscreen, that both screens exterior views and provides energy production.

One of the main explorations of the design is the maximization of flexibility within a simple arrangement of open spaces. This 2,000 square-foot residence will be capable of accommodating both large and small groups of occupants to meet the demands of current living patterns, and anticipate the inevitable changes that will occur over time. Up to ten overnight guests gather in celebration one weekend while the next, a couple will be able to make use of the entire space for relaxation and working. In the event that families emerge, both will be able to share this weekend retreat.

Project Team: Dr. Ted Kesik (building science), Geoffrey Thün, Kathy Velikov

1   Organizational Diagram
2   View of Tower Loft
3   Longitudinal Section

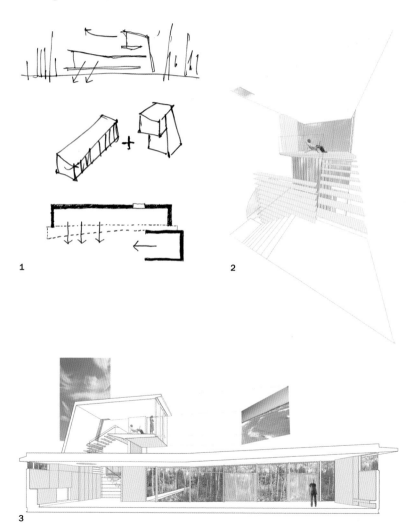

1

2

3

4   Flexible Occupancy Diagram

5   Exploded Axonometric

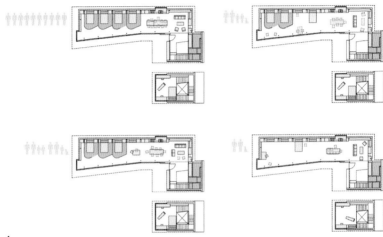

4

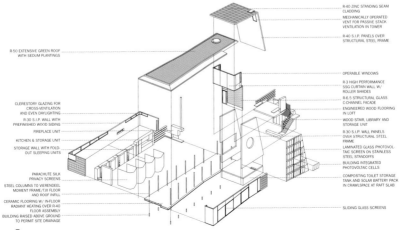

R-40 ZINC STANDING SEAM CLADDING

MECHANICALLY OPERATED VENT FOR PASSIVE STACK VENTILATION IN TOWER

R-40 S.I.P. PANELS OVER STRUCTURAL STEEL FRAME

R-50 EXTENSIVE GREEN ROOF WITH SEDUM PLANTINGS

OPERABLE WINDOWS

R-3 HIGH PERFORMANCE SSG CURTAIN WALL W/ ROLLER SHADES

R-6.5 STRUCTURAL GLASS C-CHANNEL FACADE

CLERESTORY GLAZING FOR CROSS-VENTILATION AND EVEN DAYLIGHTING

ENGINEERED WOOD FLOORING IN LOFT

R-30 S.I.P. WALL WITH PREFINISHED WOOD SIDING

WOOD STAIR, LIBRARY AND STORAGE UNIT

FIREPLACE UNIT

R-30 S.I.P. WALL PANELS OVER STRUCTURAL STEEL FRAME

KITCHEN & STORAGE UNIT

LAMINATED GLASS PHOTOVOL-TAIC SCREEN ON STAINLESS STEEL STANDOFFS

STORAGE WALL WITH FOLD-OUT SLEEPING UNITS

BUILDING INTEGRATED PHOTOVOLTAIC CELLS

PARACHUTE SILK PRIVACY SCREENS

COMPOSTING TOILET STORAGE TANK AND SOLAR BATTERY PACK IN CRAWLSPACE AT RAFT SLAB

STEEL COLUMNS TO VIERENDEEL MOMENT FRAME/TJI FLOOR AND ROOF INFILL

CERAMIC FLOORING W/ IN-FLOOR RADIANT HEATING OVER R-40 FLOOR ASSEMBLY

BUILDING RAISED ABOVE GROUND TO PERMIT SITE DRAINAGE

SLIDING GLASS SCREENS

5

6   View of Pavilion as Informal Screened Porch
7   View of Pavilion with Multiple Guests

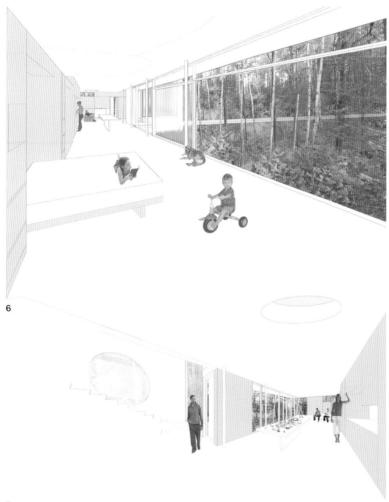

6

7

Pampas House

Pampas House was developed from within the deep contradictions of the commission to develop a sustainable polo resort community close to Buenos Aires, and engages the extremes of this lifestyle. The growing global leisure class and incidence of specialized event travel has grown at an unprecedented rate in the past decade. Many of the resulting leisure/lifestyle developments combine luxury inhabitation with unique and exotic recreational activities and are tailored to very specific clients and program combinations. This house will serve as both a site for extreme expressions of excess and boisterous pleasures, while also operating as a space for contemplative retreat from the pressures of global financial enterprise.

A twenty-foot-tall volume conceived of as a vast glass vitrine is wrapped with a C–shaped bar containing private functions for three groups of guests and linked by a long glazed ambulatory space whose mullions mirror the patterns of the pampas grasses when experienced in parallax. The exterior glazing systems of the vitrine offer an opportunity for further experimentation with a range of glazing technologies related to a group of domestic projects currently being developed within our practice. Responsive louver systems, laminated glass shear columns, and high performance film systems that are capable of displaying video projections even during full daylighting conditions comprise the primary glazed envelope.

Within the vitrine and erupting out into the courtyard formed by the private wings, a series of organic volumes house and animate the spaces of collective pleasure and spectacle. Clad alternately in double curved ply and leather panels, the interior vessels connect the wine cellar, media room and study with a sky aperture above.

Within the vitrine, these volumes enclose and deliver mechanical services in order to suppress any sign of technical systems, while operating as a highly efficient plenum space to support passive displacement air systems. Outside, these volumes are constructed from site cast and

1   Approach from Polo Fields
2   Interior at Living Vitrine

precast panels with concealed moment connections forming the pool and the polo viewing *sala* (pavilion), from which a variety of voyeuristic and entertainment activities are staged. Excess forms a background for formal tectonic and technological innovation.

Project Team: Mike Blois, Paul Raff, Colin Ripley, Matt Storus, Geoffrey Thün, Kathy Velikov

1

2

3   Situation | Circumstance | Projection
4   Longitudinal Section

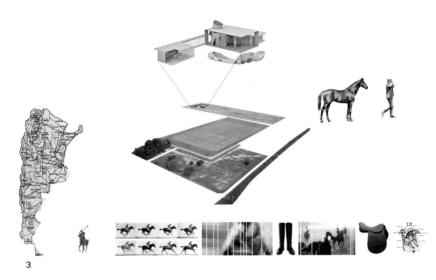

3

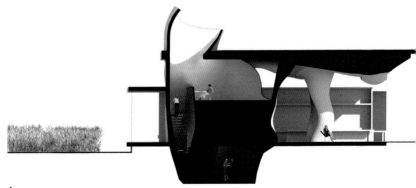

4

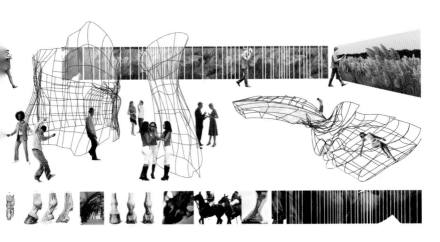

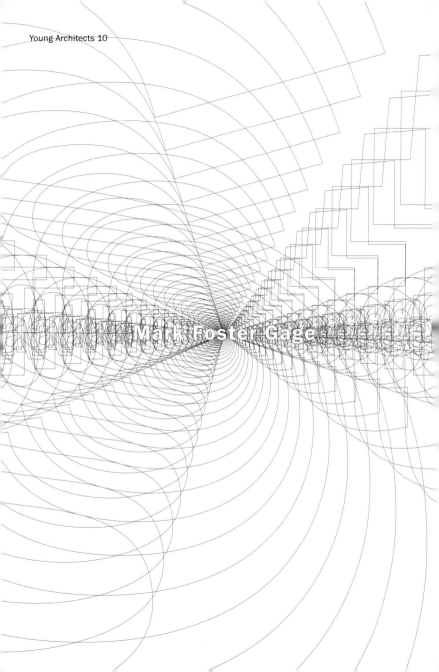

Mark Foster Gage

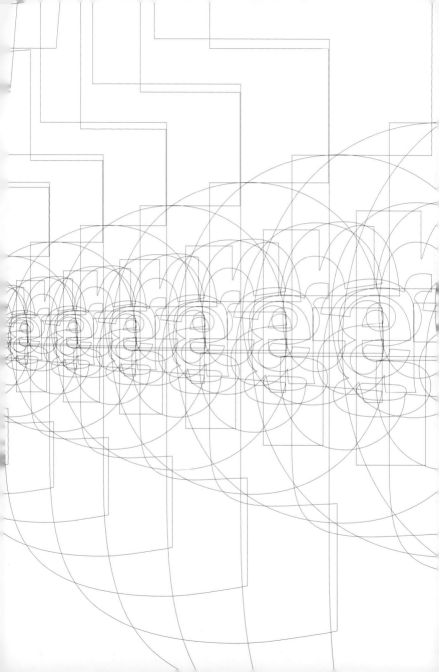

Estonian Acadamy of the Arts
+ Prototype

In the past decade architectural design has become increasingly reli-
ant on the limited form-making tools offered in standardized architectural software packages. Recent projects by Gage/Clemenceau
Architects, as well as this competition entry for the Estonian Academy
of the Arts, have actively researched the digital tools used in unrelated
design disciplines in an attempt to move beyond normally unchal-
lenged design boundaries within the architectural profession.

The facades, apertures, and large courtyard manifold openings
of this project were designed using the automotive design software
package Alias Studio, which, normally retailing at $60,000 a license, is
typically beyond the economic constraints of architectural design strategies. By creating an experimental alliance with the software manufac-
turer, Autodesk, we misused the software with the express purpose of
cross-pollinating automotive and architectural design tactics. Instead
of relying on platonic geometries, which typically guide architectural
design decisions, the facade of the Estonian Academy of the Arts is
entirely, and tautly, wrapped in what the automotive industry refers to
as "Class-A" surfaces—surfaces which produce the maximum aesthetic
effect with a minimum of mathematical description. The building contains both purely aesthetic fluid ripples and contours, as well as performative scoops, tunnels and vents that funnel fresh air to all areas
of the building—from the lobby to the interior courtyard, to the fifth
floor central manifold featured in the center of the overall composition.
Input on this process was solicited from a number of experts in various
disciplines including Chris Ruffo, the head of design visualization for
Autodesk, and Chris Bangle, the international head of design for BMW.

A large-scale prototype panel was constructed of the centralized
section of the building in order to view these surface-based geometries
at a larger, architectural scale. To be more specific, automotive design
is largely based on the placement of "break lines,"—the folds in panels
that reach along the side of a car from the front to the back. The

1   Elevation

portion of the panel above the break line reflects the sky; the portion below it reflects the road. Careful curation of the break lines, therefore, allows car designers to capitalize on the relation between the viewer, the object, the ground and the sky—which is a problem normally specific to architecture, and generally solved through massing.

This problem was addressed more specifically in the prototype panel, which was produced to research how a logic of break lines and reflection might produce a new genre of relationship between the building and its viewer. Instead of break lines running horizontal, as in a car, the break lines run vertically, allowing facade panels to fold and reflect various views of the sky and city around the site depending on one's relative location to the building. The Estonian Academy of the Arts, in this scenario, is no longer a passive urban participant.

1

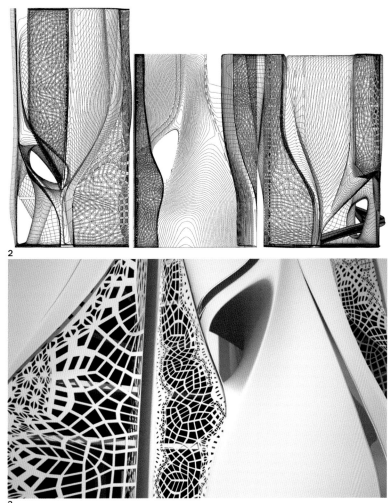

2

3

4   Perspective of Entrance
5   Elevation Perspective
6   Perspective of Elevated Courtyard

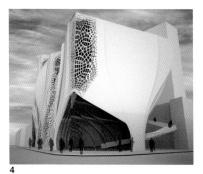

4

5

6

P.S.1/MoMA Competition

Few things are lovelier to observe than the delicate shimmer of sunlight skimming the water's surface. Delve deeper, though, and dive undersea, and suddenly this scene becomes far more seductive. Our role evolves from outside observer to inside participant. The romance of the aquatic world becomes our reality, and the white glare of direct sun blurs into a glimmering, golden, luminescent glow.

Once we're in that water, we're cooled and refreshed. Here, in the courtyard of P.S.1, we experience that same sensation of submersion and immersion, basking and bathing. Somehow, we get the best of both worlds—the relaxed state of instant relief from summer's slow burn, and the dreamy gleam of hypnotic patterns from reflecting sunrays.

Echoing the languid sways of kelp, sixteen modular structures of carbon steel tubing curve high above us. Under their undulating twists and soft contours, we're sheltered by expanded metal mesh and light metal sheets water jet-cut and folded a shading layer of rippling waves, fluid yet still, billowing and beckoning us with glints of flash and hints of form.

Industrial gold automotive paint covers these structures in their glistening entirety, while multi-colored lighting projects upward, enswathing us in the twinkling mystique of underwater awe. Sunny by day, glittering by night, small LEDs are bunched like sparkling fruit in the canopies above. We're revived by the light spray of gentle mists and replenished by several reflecting tide pools, perfect for a pure splash of summer New York magic.

1   2

3   Plan

1   Daytime Rendering   4   Detail
2   Nighttime Rendering   5   Canopy Interior (morning)

3

4

5

6 Canopy Interior (evening)

Biophelic Office

The Biophelic office, a renovation project for the Midtown Manhattan headquarters of a Ukrainian company, challenges the current thinking of sustainability in architecture. Instead of relying on performative systems that save energy and resources, this project attempts to encourage sustainability through producing an aesthetic reminder of the natural world, in a setting typically devoid of such contact. The underlying axiom was that the contemporary American corporate environment is isolated from any form of nature, and that reintroducing a living botanical environment into such a setting would function as a reminder as to what precisely is at stake in terms of sustainability.

A standard office arrangement with a perimeter of enclosed offices and interior administrative spaces is interrupted by two contoured pods. The interior of these pods are lush with live growing ferns, vines and flora—all sustained by a hydroponic growth system. In order to pass from the offices to the lobby and conference room, workers pass through these supple pods, experiencing temporary botanical relief from the more formal corporate office space environment. The presence of these lush interior garden pods not only produces a better working environment, but, in doing so, encourages sustainable behavior.

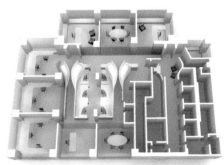

1

2

3

Stockholm Public Library

Challenging the dominance of both the poche-laden figures of classicism, and the freeform figures of modern planning—this proposal for a
library addition in Stockholm, Sweden, seeks the production of a new
species of architectural figuration. Instead of floorplates with volumes
inserted, this project places a series of elaborately contoured and
hanging programmatic "leaves" within a larger box structure. These
platforms emerge from a more standardized series of large floorplates
at the lower levels. These separate program areas are then connected
with bridges, walkways, and escalators—and are all individual territories, yet part of a visually and physically interconnected architectural whole. The twenty-first century library, in this scenario, is not an
enclave for localized and personal study, but is an active and partici-
patory environment, which encourages interaction, the exchange of
information, and the exploration of the new.

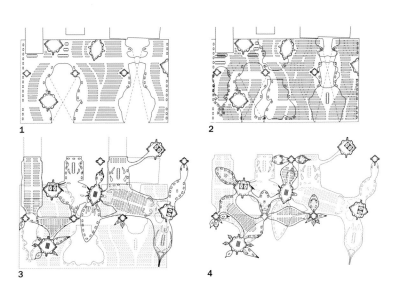

1

2

3   4

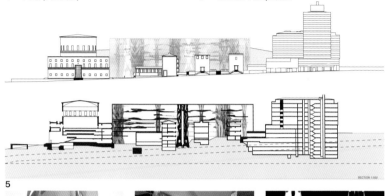

5

6

7

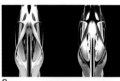

8

9

Czech National Library

One of the defining stances of twentieth-century modernism was its insistence on the material and functional legibility of geometry. The relaxation of this ambition has led to a renewed interest in the classical tendency to confuse, through the use of cornices, bases, and architraves, the transitions between floors, walls and ceilings. However, instead of relying on these classical devices, this proposal for the New National Library of the Czech Republic actively researches the twenty-first century equivalent of such geometric relaxations. Through geometric contortions, elongations and fluid attachments, floors do not only become walls, but become circulation paths, corridors, structural members, apertures, and facades. The effect is one that combines the open plan legibility of modernism with the fluid transitory articulations of classicism.

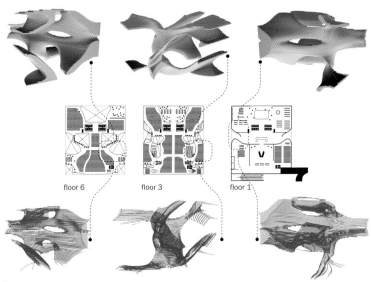

floor 6   floor 3   floor 1

2

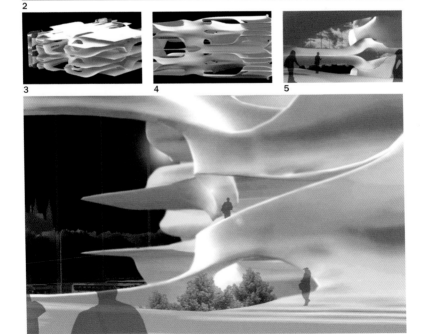

3   4   5

6

Te Wero Bridge

Spanning between two small islands adjacent to downtown Auckland,
New Zealand, the Te Wero bridge was required to function not only
as a physical link between locations, but as a visual identifier within
the city. The fluid structural canopies that define the ends of the
bridge perform the dual funciton of covering the pedestrian walkway
entrances, as well as providing a structual support from which the
tension members of the bridge are embedded. Lines of force are
drawn into the surfaces, allowing for a calculated network of cables,
reaching above, around, and under the bridge and finally securing the
forces to the ground above which the entrance seems to float.

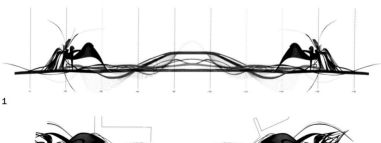

1

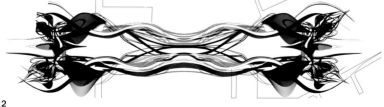

2

1   Side Elevation
2   Plan
3   Aerial Perspective
4   Aerial Perspective of Bridge Entrance

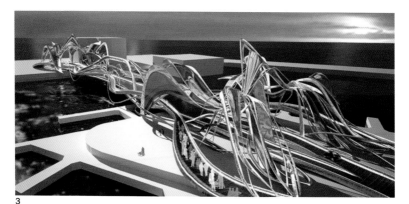

3

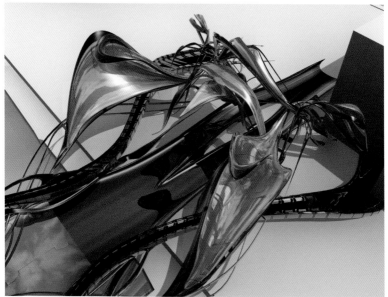

4

Residence for the *New York Times*

In late 2007 Gage/Clemenceau Architects was approached by a *New York Times* editor about collaborating with the well-known fashion photographer Ilan Rubin on a six-page pictorial for the Sunday *New York Times Magazine*. The collaboration allowed the architectural spaces to benefit from new ideas about lighting, surfaces, reflection, caustics and glow—possible only through a cross-disciplinary dialogue between photography and architecture. The end product was a series of six composite images for six high-end watches. Instead of treating the architectural spaces as backdrops for the watches, the spaces inherited the material qualities of the watches themselves, and were rendered using a rich palette of exquisite materials not typically germane to architecture, including 24-carat gold, titanium, and solid silver. The end result was a fusion of the spatial qualities of architecture, the lighting and perspectival expertise of photography and the material exquisiteness of the jewelry.

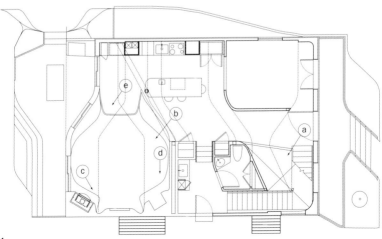

2   Living Room
3   Shelving
4   Balcony from Below
1   Plan
5   Stair

2

3

4

5

Residence in Soho

This project, for a renovation of a loft in Manhattan involved dividing a large space into smaller rooms without losing the overall ambience of a single large space. In order to accomplish this we designed a sliding screen milled using a computer-numerically-controlled (CNC) out of one-inch-thick acrylic. The screen allows for the passage of light and some views while providing the privacy necessary for a functioning bedroom area. The lighting of the screen from an embedded channel over which it hangs further illuminates the space with an aqueous glow—changing what would normally be a divisive structure within a loft into a luminous and glowing translucent feature.

1

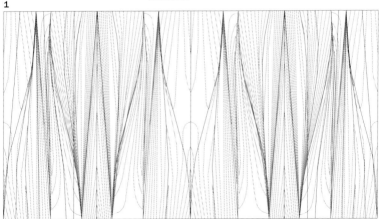

2

1   Plan
2   Screen Detail

3   CNC Milled Screen
4   Living Room
5   Bedroom

3

4

5

Residence in Chelsea

The limited size of this 350-square-foot apartment required a new
form of scalar thinking for a renovation. Instead of making large-scale
architectural decisions, the majority of the design was in the manufacturing of specific architectural textures intended to be touched.
Realizing that in a small apartment, everything is easily touched, each
surface receives a unique tactile character, providing spatial diversity
that the space itself could not provide. The black walnut surfaces of
the primary wall and custom furniture were CNC milled with a wave
pattern based on random variations of Lissajous curves. The kitchen
area, while related in palette, is a dramatically different enviroment of
smooth black corian, black glass, polished chrome, and clear acrylic.

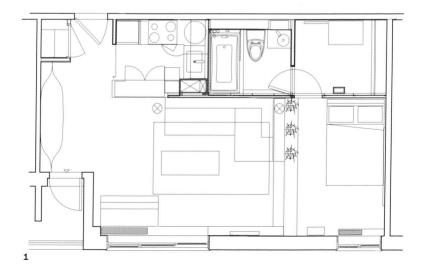

1

2   Custom Steel Desk
3   Black Translucent Glass Bathroom
4   Acrylic Kitchenette
5   Custom CNC Milled Table

1   Plan

6   Living Area

2

3

4

5

6

Residence on Central Park South

This renovation for a three-bedroom apartment and terrace on Central Park South in Manhattan provides an opportunity to reconsider the standard language of forms and surfaces typically used in residential spaces. Instead of articulating the identity of rooms by variations in color, each of the public rooms and terrace receive different language of form. The entrance foyer encrusted with massive backlit brass panels, each with an interlocking CNC water-jet-cut custom pattern which dissolves the surface from a more solid sheet at the bottom to a metallic lace at the top. The formal living room receives a pair of symmetrically contoured and torqued plaster wall surfaces that visually lead to the large outdoor terrace. The terrace itself is comprised of a fluid network of garden areas, platforms, and material changes, which gradually change character and height as they lead toward a custom chrome canopy opposite the terrace entrance.

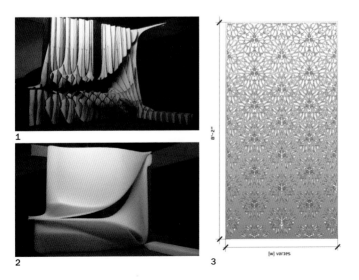

1

2

3

8'-2"

|w| varies

1   Structural Study of Torqued Wall
2   Model Study of Torqued Wall
3   Pattern for Water-jet-cut Brass Room

4   Torqued Wall Assembly
5   Water-jet-cut Brass Wall Prototype Panel
6   Living Area

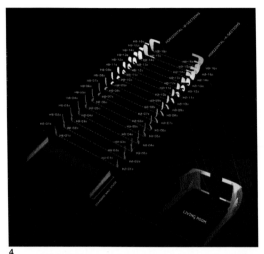

4

5

6

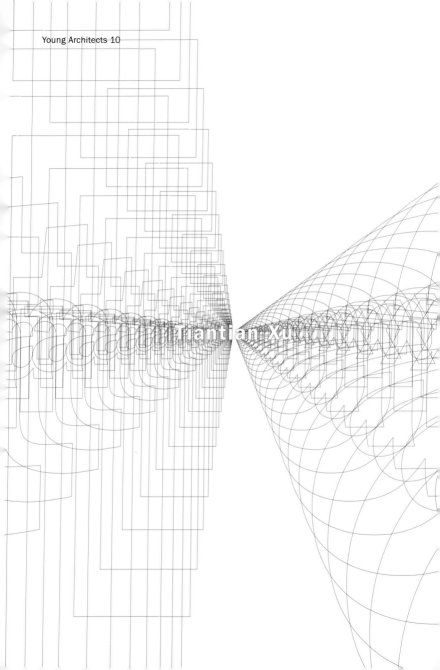

Information and Exhibition: Info Tree

Building:
As an arrival facility for visitors, this building is intended to introduce tourist attractions and geographic information for ChangBai Mountain. The program requires an exhibition space, café, gift shop, management office, and a viewing platform above 65.6 feet in elevation. So the public area is stretching up like a Changbaishan pine tree, with a continuous exhibition space starting from ground level, to a glass-wall enclosed café at the top floor, and a roof terrace with a 360-degree view. With a series of punch openings along the exhibition path, the outdoor landscape interacts with the indoor exhibition's contents and becomes a multi-dimensional introduction. The building is as informative as any road sign.

A red-painted steel core–accommodating glass elevator, outdoor steel fire stair, and vertical pile shafts function as the structure of the entire building like a tree trunk, contrasted with a dark wood building surface.

Public Space:
An open public plaza will surround the Info Tree as an information plaza adjacent to future hotel development on the west side before entering BaiXi town.

1

2

3 Concept Diagram 1
1 Concept Diagram 2   4 Plan 1
2 Concept Diagram 3   5 Plan 2

West	East	North	South

3

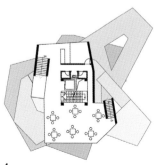
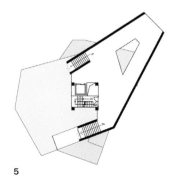

4   5

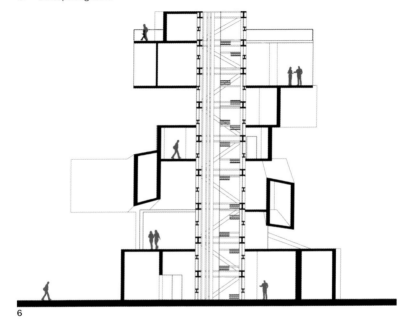

6

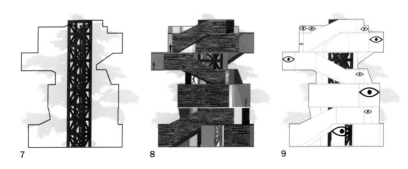

7   8   9

10

11

Sports and Leisure:
Bridging Water

Building:

With a creek-side location and a water sports program with a swimming pool, leisure pool, spa, and other supporting facilities, we spread out all the water programs on the first floor, along with an outdoor water plaza to form a water topography, with the rest of the programs crossing above like bridges. The interaction of the bridges creates vertical voids overlooking the water, channeling light and visual dialogues toward the water's surface from bridges.

Glass partitions are used inside without interrupting the visual dialogues. Water becomes an important building material here with its wave and the reflections on other surfaces when interacting with light. A glass skin is also wrapping around the exterior white walls, etched with white floral patterns. On cloudy days, the building appears as a blank white surface. When the sun comes out, a shadow of white floral patterns appears on the wall behind. The shadow pattern on the building's surface captures the movement of sun and light.

Public Space:

Most of the time, the water plaza serves as the public space; children use it as an outdoor leisure pool. In the winter, the space becomes an ice-skating rink with a view of the indoor swimming pool.

1

2

3

4

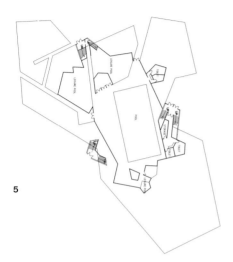

5

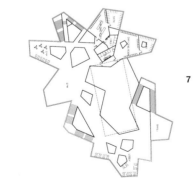

6

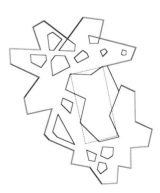

7

8   Exterior 2
9   Exterior 3

8

9

Entertainment and
Performance: The Rock

Building:
KaraOk singing and dancing has been prominent in local Korean culture. The building program of KaraOk (theater and multi-function/ballroom) requires individual spaces that do not interfere with each other or the surroundings. These spaces are regarded as rocks, with disconnection between inside and outside. The stepped floor of the theater sits on top of the lower level café and interacts with the ground to create a sunken casual performing garden, while a sloping roof for acoustical performances in each rock space unifies the roof level, transforming into a roof theater that can host outdoor rock concerts.

Concrete is used as both structure and surface material. A raw concrete surface is left without, which blends with the local rocky mountain surface.

Public Space:
The space around the Rock will be a garden with local plants. Rock is the primary landscape element in the garden.

1

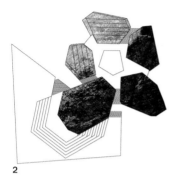

2

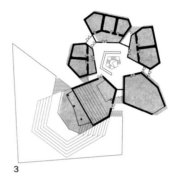

3

4

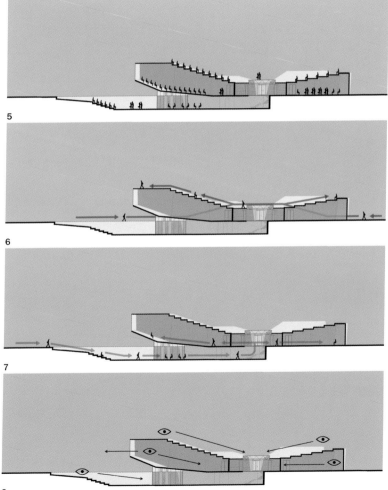

9   Concept Diagram 3
10 Exterior 2

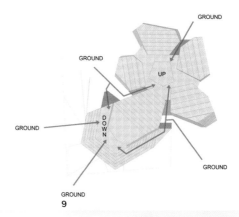

9

10

Xiaopu Culture Center

Located on an irregular former industrial lot in the well-known art village Songzhuang, Xiaopu Cultural Center is a multi-functional complex including exhibition galleries, five residency artist studios, exhibition workshop, art shop, and administration.

The programs are first carried out on this compact site as a Tangram layout, which allows the individual programmatic spaces to connect and adapt to the site. Vertically they are also distributed into dual-levels: the ground level consists of public programs including galleries, workshops, administration; the second level is occupied by artist studios and an art shop as a supporting program for the artists' residency. The public program on ground level, occupies the site with a continuous indoor circulation around a series of courtyards, while the private program of artist residencies is executed through individual volumes on the second level, allowing views from the roof terrace that travel along the red-tiled roofscape of this typical northern Chinese village.

The Tangram layout allows an intersection of studios and double-height galleries. Each artist's studio has a window to the exhibition room; visitors can have a peep into the studios where art production and presentation are both presented. The artist can be either a viewer or a part of the exhibition.

2 Concept Diagram 2

3 Exterior 1

4 Plan 1

1 Concept Diagram

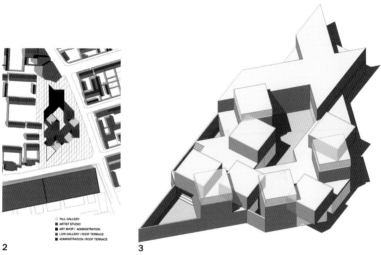

TALL GALLERY
ARTIST STUDIO
ART SHOP / ADMINISTRATION
LOW GALLERY / ROOF TERRACE
ADMINISTRATION / ROOF TERRACE

2

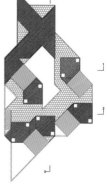

3

1. ADMINISTRATION
2. ART STORAGE
3. ENTRANCE
4. LOW GALLERY
5. TALL GALLERY
6. COURTYARD

7. ART SHOP
8. ARTIST STUDIO
9. TALL GALLERY VOID
10. ROOF TERRACE

1F PLAN   2F PLAN   ROOF PLAN

4

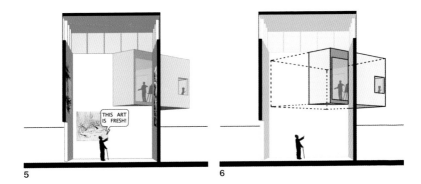

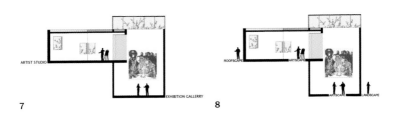

10   Exterior 2
11   Exterior 3

10

11

12

13

14

15

16

17

18

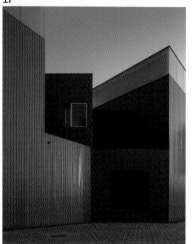

19

20

Ordos Art Museum

Ordos Art Museum is the first building of the new civic center on a
stretch of sand dunes along the lake that is dedicated as a "public
corridor" with art and cultural facilities. This 8,858 square feet of
exhibition and research space is distributed within an undulating form
with a central span lifting clear off the ground, suggesting a desert
viper winding over the dunes.

The space is conceived as one uninterrupted room with a series
of openings absorbing natural light while offering cinematic views
of the raw surroundings; the art exhibition mingles with the natural
landscape that becomes an integrated experience for views.

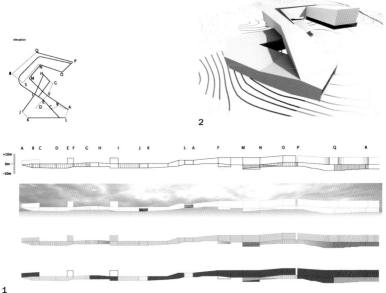

2

1

3

4

5

6

7

8

9

Jinhua Architecture Park

Zhejiang
Public Toilet

A public toilet is indeed a private space. Public Toilet is located
in Jinhua Architecture Park among sixteen other public pavilions
designed by architects from around the world and also shares space
with the work of landscape artist Ai Weiwei. This public facility is organized as individual units, maximizing privacy while minimizing land use
in the park. These units can be reproduced and installed flexibly for
future needs. The bending tube shape ensures protection and privacy,
as well as functional requirements such as ventilation and natural
lighting, without interrupting the connection between user and park.

1

1   Exterior 1   **2**   Exterior 2

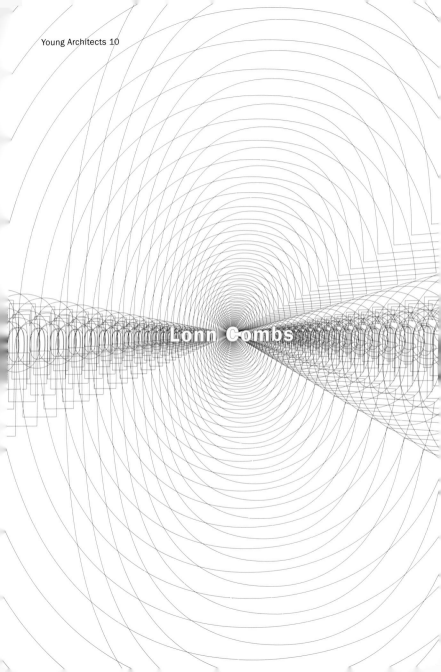

Lonn Combs

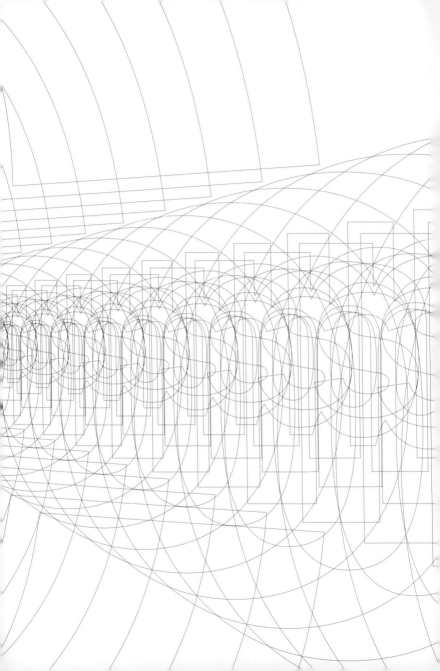

Gyeonggi-do Jeongok Prehistory Museum

Yeoncheon-gun, Gyeonggi-do, South Korea

Architecture and the Protocols of Cultural Memory

The Gyeonggi-do Jeongok Prehistory Museum is a proposal for an archive and museum for Acheulean handaxe artifacts on the sensitive site of the Acheulean era archeological excavations near the De-Militarized Zone in South Korea. The museum tells the story of prehistoric human technological innovation on the Korean peninsula that disproved the nineteenth-century world view of the dominance of early civilizations in the West.

The museum houses several hundred artifacts of Acheulean and proto-Acheulean handaxe technology in a series of suspended galleries cut diagonally through the building. The strategy of the building addresses the site condition both physically and conceptually through the suspension of the museum above the sensitive site and in the creation of an internal landscape of intimate viewing chambers for the artifacts. The structural system acts as a habitable space frame that develops into an internally porous spatial field. The field of galleries is interspersed with a series of porous light wells connecting the space of the interior to a sense of the natural environment as a background for the display of the prehistoric human artifacts.

The question of how we collect, archive, and disseminate the awareness of our past forces us to consider issues beyond its housing alone. We are confronted with the fundamental anonymity of our history, one which was before writing and one which language had no reason to retell through millennia of fleeting moments. When we acknowledge this mystery we recognize the fragility of our own cultural and technological constructs. It is in this sense that the true significance of these prehistoric tools comes into focus. The entirety of civilization flows through the material history of these remains of our past. It is not a question of lineage, rather of continuum. Yet this evidence is incomplete and we are left with remains that test the certainty of our

1   Acheulean Handaxe: Montage

postulations about the distant past. Each new excavation site not only has the potential to further elucidate the collective trace of human history but also the potential to overturn the very knowledge we seek to clarify through the spatial envelope of its classification.

Status: International Architectural Competition, 3rd Place winner.

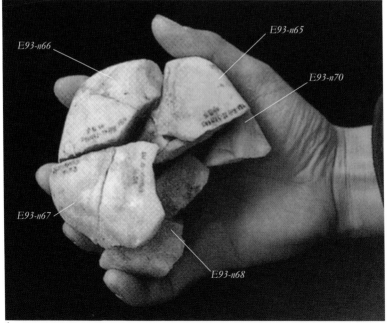

1

2 Time Line including the Acheulean Period
3 Structural Aggregation: Sequence 1
4 Structural Aggregation: Sequence 2

5 Structural Aggregation: Sequence 3
6 Structural Aggregation: Sequence 4
7 Structural Aggregation: Sequence 5

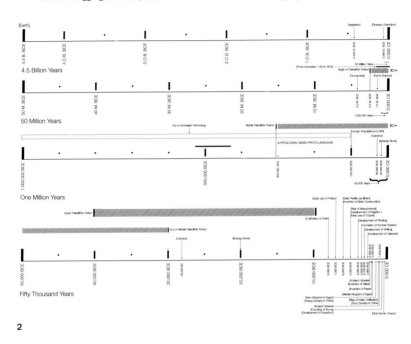

2

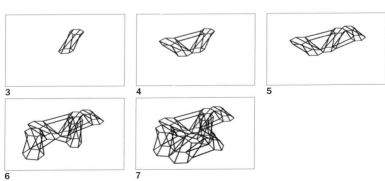

3

4

5

6

7

8   Aerial view: Prehistory Museum in the
    Landscape
9   Gallery Interior

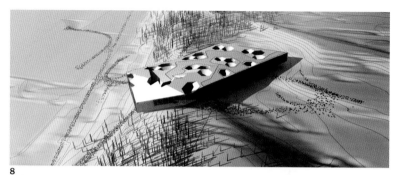

8

9

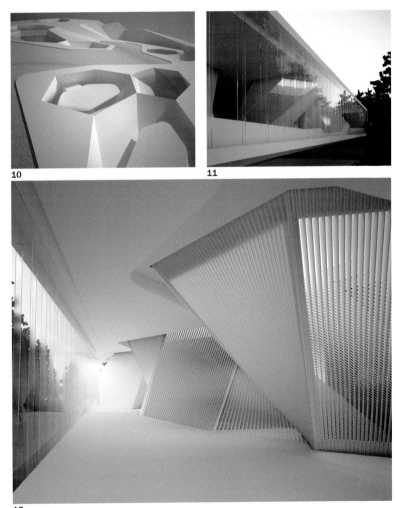

10

11

12

13 Collection Chamber Index

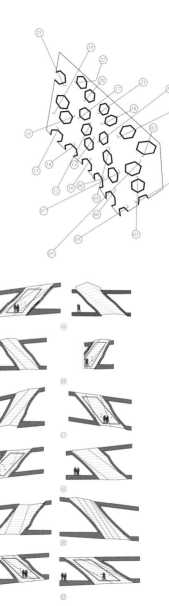

14 Main Level Plan

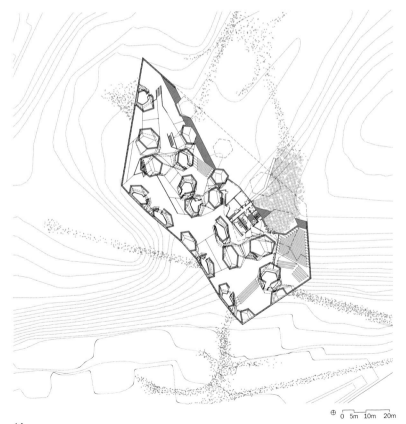

0 5m 10m 20m

15   Detail of Structural Analysis
16   Building Section

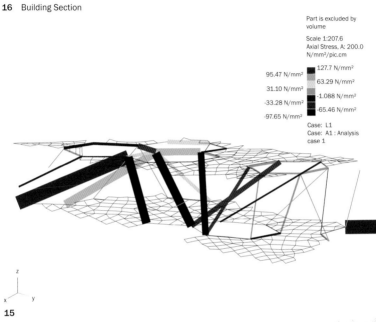

Part is excluded by volume

Scale 1:207.6
Axial Stress, A: 200.0
N/mm²/pic.cm

95.47 N/mm²   127.7 N/mm²
                     63.29 N/mm²
31.10 N/mm²
                     -1.088 N/mm²
-33.28 N/mm²
                     -65.46 N/mm²
-97.65 N/mm²

Case: L1
Case: A1 : Analysis case 1

15

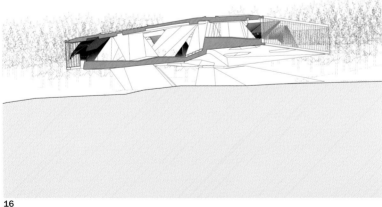

16

Hunter Douglas Light Research Studio

Research-based Academic Studio, Pratt Institute School of Architecture

The Hunter Douglas Light Research Studio is a sponsored academic material research studio that develops alternate futures from a manufactured material. The studio explores the basic environmental and cultural performance of this material. The concept of beauty, transparency, publicity, privacy, and the ability of manipulated light to induce specific categories of ambience are intrinsic to the research agenda. Full scale prototypes address the problem of leaving the wall as a decorative screed and moving into a self-supported environmental skin.

The Research Studio addresses sustainability as a larger issue of environmental performance through low-impact and non-consumptive means of environment and atmosphere modulation. As this studio deals directly with a manufactured fabric used typically as a decorative window covering and functional sun-shade device, the question of sustainable practice is involved at multiple scales of consideration within the pedagogy of the studio.

The overarching goal of the research of the studio is to return attention within the discipline of architecture to the basic conditions of affecting local atmospheres through material means, which once in operation are "non-consumptive" with respect to energy as opposed to mechanical means that are inherently consumptive with respect to energy. The fundamental pedagogic question lies in establishing the connection between the architectural surface and its cultural effect to the architectural surface and its atmospheric effect. To this end the students developed strategies of material manipulation that modulated the affect of light, temperature and acoustic isolation.

Central to the studio was the question of how one could move the material performances into new applications of architectural space, thus expanding the potential range from window covering to architectural partitions of space with embedded light and temperature control qualities. The research included developing a structural weave that integrates into the lightweight fabric in order to achieve free-standing material configurations.

1   Installation View

Studio Credits:
Instructors: Lonn Combs and Mark Parsons
Digital Consultant: Kyle Steinfeld

Pratt Architecture Students:
Daniel Breitner, Joanna Cheung, Jason Gross, Laura Haak, Matthew Howard, Peter VanHage, Wilmer Zamora

Pratt Interior Design Students:
Stephanie Benete, OhYoung Kwon, Ji Hyun Lee, Jooyoun Lee, Cheng Feng Lin, Hannah Oh, Andrei Shiryaev, Hannah Wee

1

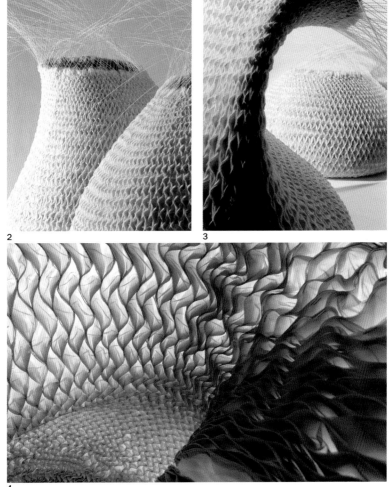

2

3

4

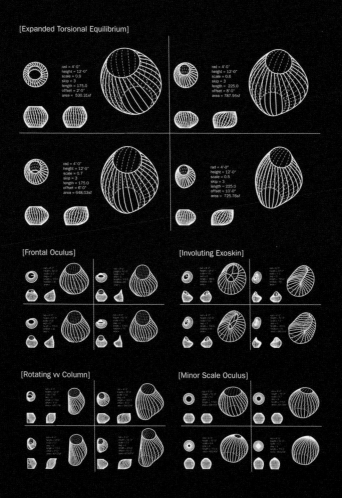

[Expanded Torsional Equilibrium]

[Frontal Oculus]

[Involuting Exoskin]

[Rotating vv Column]

[Minor Scale Oculus]

Anthology of spatial surface type

Hunter Douglas Light Research Studio
Matter-Sphere Atmospheres

6

7

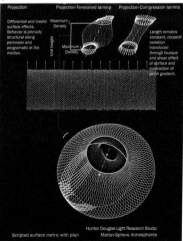

8

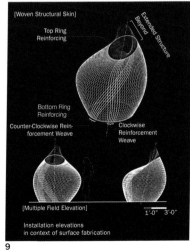

9

10

IAH Airport Parking Facility

Houston, Texas

Architecture and the Spatial Protocols of Contemporary Travel

The parking facility for the Bush Intercontinental Airport Houston (IAH) is a private commercial extension of the airport's infrastructure and economic fabric. The project functions as an intermodal link from automobile travel to the airport terminal.

During the last decade the IAH has expanded at an accelerated rate accommodating an ever-growing culture of commercial air travel. In tandem with this development the surrounding rural landscape has developed into a transitional zone of commercial development and infrastructure responding directly to the economies of travel. As a virtual reciprocal action to the airport's expansion, these transitional zones have seen layers of private commercial development respond to and feed from the airport as an economic magnet.

The IAH Airport Parking Facility is a direct programmatic response as a participant in this secondary economy of the transitional zone outlying the airport's municipal boundaries. In this sense the project becomes part of the larger infrastructural condition of the airport and requires an architectural response that addresses multiple scales of landscape, physically and virtually, both at the scale of air travel, and at the scale of the commercial infrastructural landscape of the larger economic ecology of airport.

Two primary values of landscape and threshold express and reinforce the ritual of travel throughout the project. The volume of program dedicated to the housing of the automobile allows an architectural expression of landscape on a conceptual and figural level, both from the air and in the horizon. The open air structures propose an environment of over-scaled waiting halls that dispatches and receives the traveler. The Administration Building operates at another scale to form the initial and final architectural threshold of travel, bringing the body, via the vehicle, into a pressured spatial relationship with the building through its one hundred-foot-long linear cantilever.

1   Administration Building

1

2   Administration Building
3   Administration Building: Section   4   Administration Building: Ground Plan

2

3

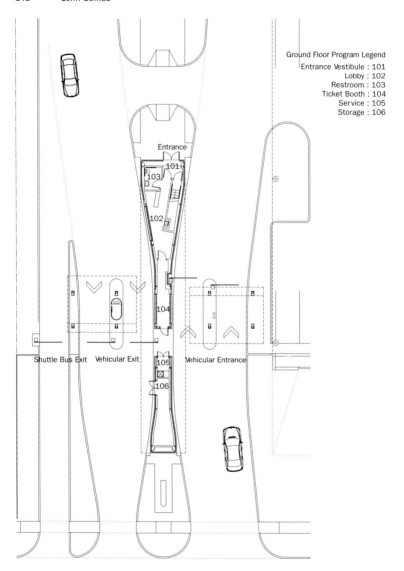

Ground Floor Program Legend

Entrance Vestibule : 101
Lobby : 102
Restroom : 103
Ticket Booth : 104
Service : 105
Storage : 106

Entrance

Shuttle Bus Exit   Vehicular Exit   Vehicular Entrance

0'   10'   20'   40'

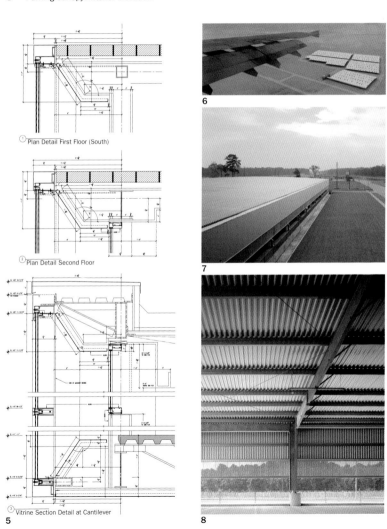

① Plan Detail First Floor (South)

② Plan Detail Second Floor

③ Vitrine Section Detail at Cantilever

5   8

9   Parking Canopy: Interior Field
10 Parking Canopy: Front Elevation

9

10

The Mill Center for the Arts

Hendersonville, North Carolina

The Architectural Surface of Social Life

The strength of any community hinges upon the success of its public institutions. The social function of the public courthouse and the town square
as the cornerstone of public life in the early twentieth century has arguably
been transferred to the public art institutions of the early twenty-first
century. In the case of the Mill Center for the Arts, the idea of a performing
arts venue merges with the community center to form a dynamic locus of
contemporary cultural identity for the local populace and the larger region.
The Mill Center design extends the topic of "performance center" into the
secondary and tertiary civic roles of the building as a community center.
The architectural expression is a celebration of both the cultural performance of the everyday and the exceptional performance of art.

The Mill Center presents an ambitious program of a multipurpose
performance hall and studio theater with a children's museum, conference center, art gallery, artist studios, and classrooms. The design strategy recognizes the distinction between performance and spectator as
one of geography, and in doing so seeks to occupy the conceptual space
of the proscenium as a fluid temporary boundary that is in constant nego-
tiation between the multifaceted event structures of the program and the
larger townscapes social milieu.

Through a precise articulation of the value of organized performance,
threading with the idea of cultural performance, the program conflates to
reinforce the very idea of community and the role of the arts within its identity. An architectural play in the skin and envelope articulate the conceptual
approach to the program as an evolution of surface, form and environment.
The building skin accommodates programmatic disturbances as a visual
display of activity and local performance. The roofscape evolves toward a
specificity of environmental performance by allowing natural light, ventilation and a thickened thermal transition zone in summer and winter alike.

Status: NEA Sponsored Architectural Competition: Awarded Finalist (1 of 3)

1   Working Model: Roofscape
2   Working Model: Sectional View
3   Entrance Condition

1

2

3

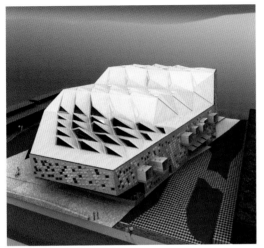

4

5

6

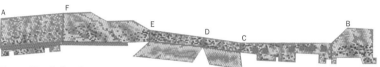

Flattened Facade Elevation

Panel type legend

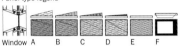

Window
detail   A   B   C   D   E   F
7

Facade Field

LEGEND

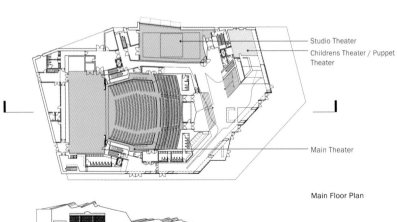

Studio Theater

Childrens Theater / Puppet
Theater

Main Theater

Main Floor Plan

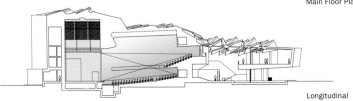

Longitudinal

8

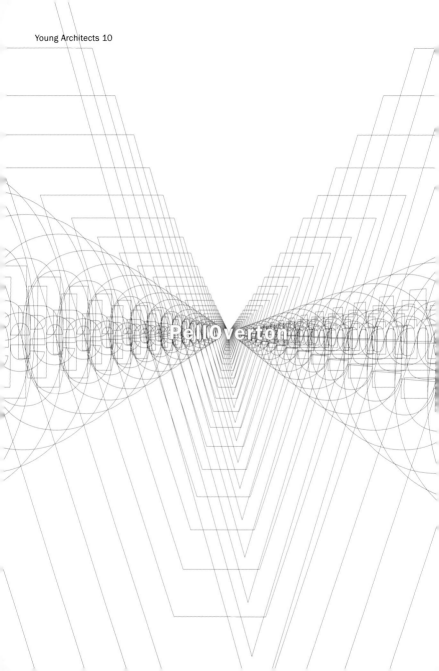

Pell Overton

Perch House
North Carolina (2008)

The siting of the Perch House was challenged by a mandate from the clients to provide views in two opposing directions: towards the mountains to the West, and down into the valley of the property to the East. In response, the house was designed as a pair of stacked volumes—each opening to a different view—with one perched above the other and supported by the stair and the fireplace which act as structural cores.

Given the strong visual presence of the white birch trees that cover the property, we became interested in situating the house into its surroundings through a shared graphic sensibility with the site. To that end, the placement and size of mullions and full-height glass framed below the floor line produces a visual flattening of the exterior, rarefying the view of the outdoors from within as a pictorial condition. While the glazing systems are framed with irregularly spaced thick concrete surrounds and aluminum frames that mimic the width and spacing of the birch trees just beyond, the solid walls invert the reading of mullion-as-tree through a series of narrow, vertical windows that allow morning light to filter into the bedroom as through the branches of the surrounding birch forest.

Project credits: Ben Pell, Tate Overton, Katy Seaman

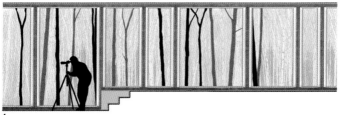

1

2   The White Birch Trees that Cover the Site

3   Diagram of Vertical Windows at Closed
        End of Upper Volume

1   Silhouette of Concrete Surrounds and
        Layers of Birch Trees Beyond

4   Looking up Toward the Open End of the
        Lower Volume

2

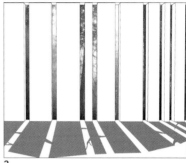

3

4

5   Bedroom Suite Volume, Looking Southwest
     Toward the Mountains
6   Morning Light Filtered through Vertical
     Strip Windows at the East End

7   Stair Ascending to Upper Bedroom Suite
     and Concrete Surrounds at Lower Volume
     Windows

5

6

7

8 House Sections
9 Two Stacked Volumes with Open Faces in
Opposing Directions

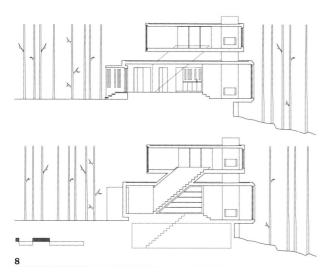

8

9

Passive Aggressive
New York (2008)

This installation was designed for an invited exhibition of our work at a Lower East Side gallery and attempts to generate visual and material affinities between the surfaces of the gallery, the work on view, and the occupants—essentially operating in two different registers: Passive and Aggressive. The Aggressive mode of the exhibit brings the figural qualities of the installation to the foreground through four wall types— assembled, printed, planted, and reflective—which were allowed to overlap either visually or physically throughout the gallery to establish a sense of movement and a network of affinities. For example: peace lilies growing through the planted wall were reproduced as graphic patterns that would glow through the printed wall; or the mirror finish stainless steel bar and folded planes of the dropped mylar ceiling, which would conflate the red glow of the printed wall with the textured surface of the assembled wall. In its Passive mode, the installation serves as background for other activities and exhibits in the space by providing both mood and discrete shape to the long, narrow gallery. The installation reconceives the gallery as two spaces, small and large, which can function separately or continuously, aiding the curation of simultaneous programming in the gallery.

Project credits: Ben Pell, Tate Overton, Mellis Haward

1   2

1   *The Wreck of the Hope*, Caspar David
Friedrich (1824)

2   *A Thicket of Deer at the Stream of Plaisir-
Fontaine*, Gustave Courbet (1866)

3   Passive: The Patterned Background of Cut
and Printed Botanical Figures

4   Birdseye Plan

3

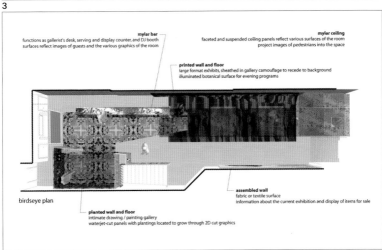

mylar bar
functions as gallerist's desk, serving and display counter, and DJ booth
surfaces reflect images of guests and the various graphics of the room

mylar ceiling
faceted and suspended ceiling panels reflect various surfaces of the room
project images of pedestrians into the space

printed wall and floor
large format exhibits, sheathed in gallery camouflage to recede to background
illuminated botanical surface for evening programs

assembled wall
fabric or textile surface
information about the current exhibition and display of items for sale

birdseye plan

planted wall and floor
intimate drawing / painting gallery
waterjet-cut panels with plantings located to grow through 2D cut graphics

4

5   Adhesive Vinyl Prints over Aluminum,
    CNC Water-jet-cut with Matching Botanical
    Patterns
6   Printed Wall: Passive / Aggressive

7   Aggressive: The Printed Wall Illuminated
    from Behind

5

6

159   PellOverton

8

9

10

Walldrobe/Wearpaper
(2005)

The Walldrobe / Wearpaper system was designed to operate alternately as a graphic appliqué for the home and as a complete, demountable clothing system. These roles are put into tension through two parallel but competing strategies with regards to performance: a logic of pattern (independent and unconditioned by its application) and a logic of the garment (specific and proportioned to the body). The collection merges conventional template-based tailoring with contemporary digital fabrication technologies, namely CNC lasercutting. Multiple garments are arranged on a single 18"x32" sheet of deerskin leather, enabling one of two garments, in one of three sizes, to be produced from a single pre-cut hide. The lines of the rejected, uncut garments are etched on the surface of the selected piece, producing a flat and complex composition of unused geometries and snap markings. The cut pieces and surrounding residual panels are fitted with nickel-finished wire snaps, which are used to snap the garment pieces together into clothing and onto the wall as wallpaper. The kit-of-parts production enables the Walldrobe / Wearpaper to grow to the extents of a room, moving incrementally like widths of wallpaper. When mounted on the wall, the collection presents a continuous and abstract graphic. While the compositional logic of this pattern isn't legible in its flattened arrangement, the cut and score lines of the garments provide clues about the alternative configurations of the panels.

Project credits: Ben Pell with Theodore Grothe

1   2

1 Dressmaking Patterns (c. 1950)
2 W/W on Display, Syracuse (March, 2005)
3 Ordering, Installing, and Assembling

4 Cutting Files for the Shirt and Shorts Panels
5 Hanging Panels and Assembled Garments
6 Details of Skirt and Shirt
7 Back of Shirt, Etched with Uncut Garments

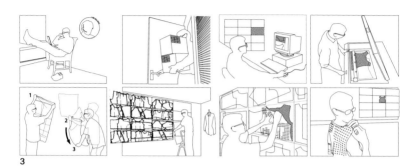

3

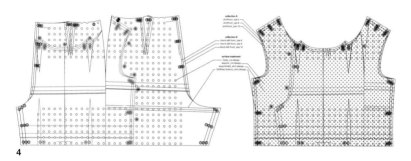

4

5

6

7

Studies for a Strip Mall

Stamford, Connecticut (2005)

For this commissioned study for a commercial strip in Stamford, we were asked to consider new visions for the mall which would add interest and value to the site without interrupting the operations of the current tenants of the building. The client's family purchased the property in the 1950s, since which time the city of Stamford has developed into a bustling commuter city. Taking cues from the cultural and physical landscape around the site, which sits at the intersection of bus, train, and car transit, the project was envisioned as a representation of Stamford as a city of movement. Appropriating the vinyl wrap-a-round advertising tactics of the buses which frequently pass the site, a new billboard-sized structure is wrapped with a blurred image of Stamford as seen from a moving commuter train. The installation is constructed of clear, 4x8 corrugated fiberglass panels which have been rotated to allow the corrugations to direct rainwater run-off away from the storefronts below. The new facelift for the mall begins just above the doors of the retail storefronts below, and draws significant visibility and attention to the previously neglected site. During the day, as cars and buses wait frozen at the congested traffic light just across from our site, they are greeted by a large-scale image of movement. At night a series of fluorescent tube lights illuminate the image from behind, accenting it with streaks of color, suggestive of the speeding taillights and headlights of the four-lane roadway below.

Project credits: Ben Pell and Tate Overton

1

1 Elevation of the Strip Mall with its New Face

2 Commuters Waiting at the Light, Looking at an Image of Movement
3 The Existing Strip Mall
4 Image by Day
5 The Installation at Night

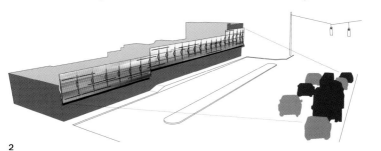

2

3

4

5

h/EDGE
Designing the High Line competition (2003)

Whereas the situation of Central Park into the heart of the city required the allocation of 843 acres from the plan of New York, the elevated platform of the High Line is a tabula rasa for the construction of a new vertical park, one which reconsiders the artificial, picturesque promenades of Central Park, and establishes a 37-block-long green base to the West Side skyline of Manhattan.

h/EDGE is a self-sustaining, five-story garden structure, belonging to the traditions of espalier and aerial hedge design. The structure does not predetermine the programming of public space, but rather houses a series of fully enclosed gardens that are open to the public. Each garden showcases different, featured plant species found along the existing High Line platform, creating unique environments for a variety of public activities. Non-corrosive metal screens of varying sizes and porosity are secured to the frames of the five stacked platforms. Each screen type provides different degrees of aperture for both the entrance of sunlight and rainwater, and the natural extension of growth from within the volume. The architecture of this proposal is therefore one that emerges from the positioned patterns of stimulated growth, allowing the natural beauty of the High Line to continue to evolve as a predictable, yet uncontrolled nature.

Project credits: Ben Pell and Tate Overton

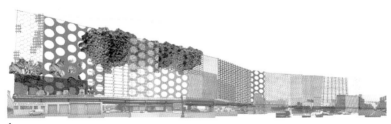

2

3

4

5

83% porosity

75% porosity

55% porosity

6   83% porosity   40%
                          porosity

98% porosity

7

8

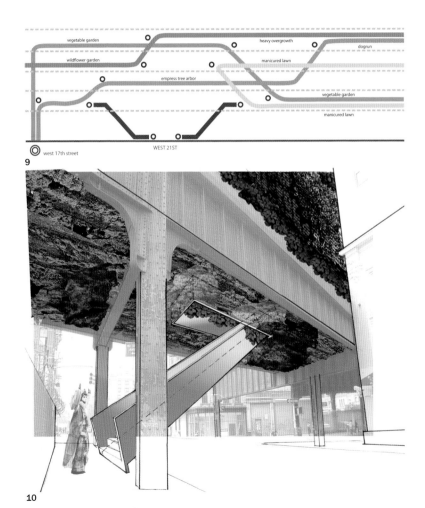

9

10

the mountain hu(n)t

Palisades Glacier Mountain Hut competition (2003)

With renewed consideration being given to North American traditions of camping and outdoor adventure, this project proposes an innovative and customizable prototype: a pre-fabricated assembly that is at once globally deployable and environmentally specific. The "mountain hu(n)t" offers an architectural proposal which combines the centralized functionality of the European great camp or mountain hut with the physical impermanence of the American individuated tent-style campground.

First and foremost, "the mountain hu(n)t" is designed to go away. It is a fully contained, thermally insulated and self-sustaining complex, submerged beneath the ground and assembled from pre-cast concrete shell units (PCS), each augmented with a range of auxiliary functions. After properly excavating and waterproofing the site, PCS components are linked together into a continuous, circular underground facility, 300 meters in diameter. The subterranean complex is expressed at grade as two parallel channels—one that brings light into the common spaces below, and one that collects rainwater and vents the underground passage. These channels are capped with customizable inserts (INS), adopting moments of difference from the particularities of the natural environment and operating in the landscape similarly to traditional trailmarkers. Through the identification and appropriation of indigenous difference—in the form of animal, vegetable or mineral—INS variations produce a range of visual effects as a means of revealing the project in its surroundings. Activating the visual ciphers of a particular biome—weaknesses in camouflage, such as the reflection in the desert, or signs of warning, such as the poisonous frog—the project translates these moments into environment-specific, architectural effects.

Project credits: Ben Pell and Tate Overton

1   Disappearing Act
2   Section of the Maginot Line (c.1917)
3   Mock-up of the *Grasslands* Mountain Hu(n)t
4   Typical Circular Site Plan
5   Parallel Channels

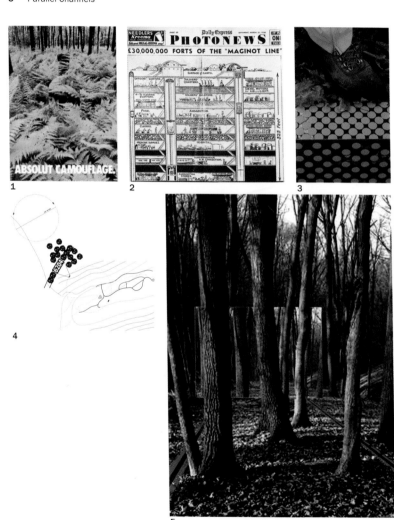

6   INS 012 – *Amazon Rainforest*
7   INS 057 - *Saharan Desert*
8   INS 006 – *East Village, NYC*

6

INS - 012 AMAZON RAINFOREST
COLOR IMPREGNATED FIBERGLASS

This insert adopts the coloring of the Amazon autumnalis lilacina, commonly known as the Parrot; indigenous to the tropical rainforest environments throughout South America

7

INS - 057 SAHARAN DESERT
REFLECTIVE METAL

The Desert insert takes its cue from the classic moments of accidentally exposing a secret position in the desert by inadvertently capturing the blazing sun in the reflection of a mirror or shiny metal instrument.

8

INS - 006 EAST VILLAGE, NYC
FLUORESCENT LIGHTING

This insert responds to the typical priority given to the vertical surface through aperture and signage, resulting in the darkness of the urban floor. The inset fluorescent tubes produce an alternative, luminous experience for the urban adventurer.

9   The Pre-Cast Concrete Shell Units (PCS) are
        Globally Deployable…

10 …While the Insert Sleeves (INS) are Envi-
        ronmentally Specific

11 Section through a Typical Mountain Hu(n)t
        Installation

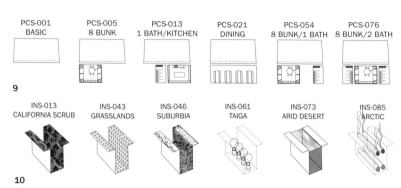

| PCS-001
BASIC | PCS-005
8 BUNK | PCS-013
1 BATH/KITCHEN | PCS-021
DINING | PCS-054
8 BUNK/1 BATH | PCS-076
8 BUNK/2 BATH |

9

| INS-013
CALIFORNIA SCRUB | INS-043
GRASSLANDS | INS-046
SUBURBIA | INS-061
TAIGA | INS-073
ARID DESERT | INS-085
ARCTIC |

10

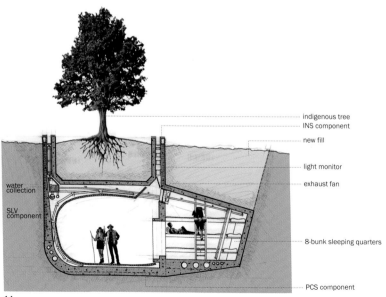

indigenous tree
INS component

new fill

light monitor

exhaust fan

water collection

SLV component

8-bunk sleeping quarters

PCS component

11

Pattern Lab

Urban Assembly School of Design and Construction, New York (2007)

The design for the Science Lab at the UASDC developed from our first meeting with our student clients, who were clear in their grievances: the current lab is composed of mostly unusable or broken cabinetry and equipment, there is no safe or convenient place to store jackets and bags during lab time, and the bland, pea-green-colored walls of the room are uninspiring. Given that the School Construction Authority had restricted our work to finishes, we considered the ways in which "finish" could be reconceptualized.

Looking to existing conditions of the room for clues as to how the lab would be used, we began with the only two signs of life on the walls: a tattered poster of the standard Periodic Table and a graphic placard with chemical safety instructions. Using the shape of the Periodic Table as a building block, the project evolved into a thick, programmed wallpaper—an applied pattern which could organize the various functions we needed in a continuous but varied three-dimensional surface. The mix of activities consisted of storage for large and small equipment, improved desk and overhead lighting, individual whiteboards at each workstation, and graphics that could inspire students to think about the role of science beyond the classroom. While the overall shape of the Periodic Table repeats from station to station, the mix and locations of the various programs shift to create unique combinations at each station, blurring the boundaries of the repeat. Ultimately this thick wallpaper system transforms each desk area into a self-contained working/teaching station, where students can access stored materials specific to their lesson, record their observations, and identify their work with the vast world of science.

Project credits: Ben Pell, Tate Overton, Miriam Peterson, Katy Seaman

1   The Standard Periodic Table
2   Science Graphics to be Included
3   Translating into a Workable Shape
4   Overall Perspective of the New and
    Improved Lab

1

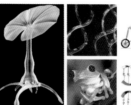

2

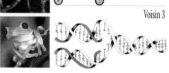

3

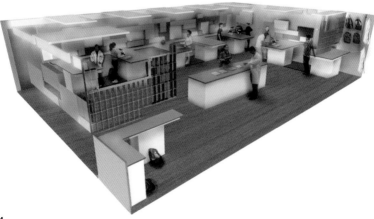

4

5   Typical Pattern Width / Section through
    the Thickened Layers of Finish
6   Open Screens at Either Entry Introduce the
    Pattern

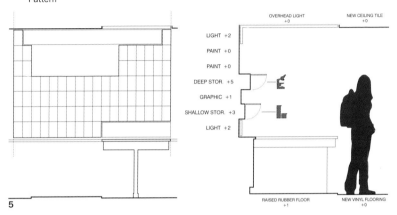

OVERHEAD LIGHT
+0

NEW CEILING TILE
+0

LIGHT   +2

PAINT   +0

PAINT   +0

DEEP STOR.   +5

GRAPHIC   +1

SHALLOW STOR.   +3

LIGHT   +2

RAISED RUBBER FLOOR
+1

NEW VINYL FLOORING
+0

5

6

7   New Programmed Finish Creates a
        Complete Teaching / Working station at
        Each Desk

8   Diagram of Components of the New Lab

7

deseek level and overhead lighting
transluscent plexi-glass fixtures at desk level and Barisol ceiling
panels over each desk provide both general and task lighting

deep and shallow storage
designed to accommodate various lab materials used by
students on a daily basis: goggles, beakers, microscopes, etc.

whiteboards
located between each desk, provide place for students
and teacher to keep notes on current assignments

workstations
two-person desks equipped with gas jets and sinks
lower cabinets for locked storage of lab materials

open screen
establishes basic compositional pattern upon entering the room separates lab
area from coat and bag check, while keeping personal property visible and safe

8